# The Governance Report 2015
Hertie School of Governance

OXFORD

# The Governance Report 2015

UNIVERSITY PRESS

UNIVERSITY PRESS

Great Clarendon Street, Oxford, OX2 6DP,
United Kingdom

Oxford University Press is a department of the University of Oxford.
It furthers the University's objective of excellence in research, scholarship,
and education by publishing worldwide. Oxford is a registered trade mark of
Oxford University Press in the UK and in certain other countries

© Hertie School of Governance 2015

The moral rights of the authors have been asserted

First Edition published in 2015

All rights reserved. No part of this publication may be reproduced, stored in
a retrieval system, or transmitted, in any form or by any means, without the
prior permission in writing of Oxford University Press, or as expressly permitted
by law, by licence or under terms agreed with the appropriate reprographics
rights organization. Enquiries concerning reproduction outside the scope of the
above should be sent to the Rights Department, Oxford University Press, at the
address above

You must not circulate this work in any other form
and you must impose this same condition on any acquirer

Published in the United States of America by Oxford University Press
198 Madison Avenue, New York, NY 10016, United States of America

British Library Cataloguing in Publication Data
Data available

Library of Congress Cataloguing in Publication Data
Data Available

ISBN 978-0-19-873431-4

Links to third party websites are provided by Oxford in good faith and
for information only. Oxford disclaims any responsibility for the materials
contained in any third party website referenced in this work.

# Table of Contents

Preface ... 7
Acknowledgements ... 9
List of Tables, Figures, and Boxes ... 11
List of Acronyms ... 12

I. **Introduction: Exploratory Governance in the Euro Crisis** ... 13
   MARK DAWSON, HENRIK ENDERLEIN, *and* CHRISTIAN JOERGES

II. **The Euro as a Showcase for Exploratory Governance: Why There Are No Simple Answers** ... 25
   HENRIK ENDERLEIN

III. **The Euro Crisis and Its Transformation of EU Law and Politics** ... 41
   MARK DAWSON

IV. **The Legitimacy *Problématique* of Economic Governance in the EU** ... 69
   CHRISTIAN JOERGES

V. **Governance Indicators** ... 95
   LIAM MCGRATH

VI. **Outlook: Where Do the EU and the EMU Go from Here?** ... 117
   MARK DAWSON, HENRIK ENDERLEIN, *and* CHRISTIAN JOERGES

Appendix: The Main Treaties of the European Union ... 127
References ... 133
About the Contributors ... 146

# Preface

The *Governance Report* 2015 is the third in this annual series about the changing conditions of governance, the challenges and opportunities involved, and the implications and recommendations that present themselves to analysts and policy-makers.

The Governance Report is an interdisciplinary effort to examine the state of the art of governance. In doing so, it enlists experts from the Hertie School of Governance in Berlin as well as from other institutions. Special attention is paid to institutional designs and approaches, changes, and innovations that both state and non-state actors have adopted in response to the shifts that have been occurring–and, in this year's edition, in response to the fiscal and economic crises experienced in the European Union, especially the eurozone.

The results are available in an annual series that includes this compact report and an edited companion volume, both published by Oxford University Press, and a dedicated website at www.governancereport.org. Together, these various outputs and outlets are designed to provide both policy-makers and analysts with ideas, knowledge, and tools to consider and implement policies and programmes that lead to better solutions to public problems.

Launched in February 2013, the first edition examines the challenges of financial and fiscal governance, proposes a new paradigm of responsible sovereignty for tackling global issues, highlights selected governance innovations, and introduces a new generation of governance indicators. In the 2014 edition, the focus turns to administrative capacity in OECD countries and how governments and their public administrations coordinate branches of the state, regulate markets, deliver services, implement policy, and make sense of increasingly complex tasks through the use of knowledge and analysis. It questions how much 'muscle' is left during the current 'age of austerity' after waves of reforms that have changed the architecture of the state.

The 2015 edition again picks up many of these topics and examines them in the context of the European Union, especially since the onset of the eurozone crisis. In keeping with the Report's interdisciplinary approach, Hertie School faculty members Mark Dawson, Henrik Enderlein, and Christian Joerges apply the lenses of their respective academic disciplines to assess where the European integration project is now, where it should go, and alternatives for getting there. In the process, the lead authors highlight the practical and political trade-offs facing governance actors in dealing with the eurozone crisis, the interdependence and heterogeneities of the EU's economies and polities, and the externalities resulting from judgements and decisions made at the nation-state level.

Unlike previous editions, the 2015 edition does not include a separate chapter on governance innovations. Instead, each of the chapters authored by a Hertie School faculty member highlights economic, institutional, and legal innovations that emerged before and during the eurozone crisis. Ultimately, the EU itself is an unprecedented innovation that continues to unfold.

Finally, the Governance Report series seeks to provide evidence to support decision-making processes by developing a new generation of indicators. The dashboards in which we present data on a variety of variables either taken from existing sources or collected by our indicators team provide a wealth of information for policy-makers and researchers that can be extracted and analysed according to the issue or question at hand. In the first edition, we offer the rationale for introducing a new set of indicators into a veritable 'indicators industry' and a sampling of the kinds of useful analyses that could be performed. For the 2014 edition, the set of dashboards is expanded to incorporate variables that focus on administrative capacity. Sample analyses illustrate the many possible applications and uses of this new generation of governance indicators. The 2015 edition, focusing on EU member states, offers a dashboard of various economic and public opinion variables and suggests ways of tracing convergence or divergence on those variables and examining other key relationships. The dashboards and analytical tools described in the Report are also available at www.governancereport.org.

Work on future editions focusing on infrastructure governance, metropolitan governance, and other topics has already begun. We invite your comments and suggestions at www.governancereport.org.

 Helmut K. Anheier and Regina A. List
 Berlin, January 2015

# Acknowledgements

Many people have been involved in developing this edition of *The Governance Report*, in addition to the authors of the various chapters.

First, we would like to thank the members of our International Advisory Committee:

| | |
|---|---|
| CRAIG CALHOUN | London School of Economics |
| WILLIAM ROBERTS CLARK | University of Michigan |
| JOHN COATSWORTH | Columbia University |
| ANN FLORINI | Singapore Management University & Brookings Institution |
| GEOFFREY GARRETT | University of Pennsylvania |
| MARY KALDOR | London School of Economics |
| EDMUND J. MALESKY | Duke University |
| HENRIETTA MOORE | University College London |
| WOODY POWELL | Stanford University |
| BO ROTHSTEIN | Quality of Government Institute, University of Gothenburg |
| SHANKER SATYANATH | New York University |
| JAMES VREELAND | Georgetown University |
| KENT WEAVER | Georgetown University |
| ARNE WESTAD | IDEAS, London School of Economics |
| MICHAEL ZÜRN | Wissenschaftszentrum Berlin |

In the process of developing the Report, we convened a workshop in May 2014 of experts and contributors to the companion edited volume that will be published by Oxford University Press later in 2015. We are grateful for the inputs received from participants in the workshop, including Michelle Everson (Birkbeck College), Sergio Fabbrini (LUISS Guido Carli), Alicia Hinarejos (Cambridge University), Daniel Innerarity (Instituto Governanza Democrática), Claus Offe (Hertie School), Jean Pisani-Ferry (Hertie School), Loukas Tsoukalis (University of Athens), and Albert Weale (University College London).

We also thank the Hertie School community, especially the many faculty members who have contributed their ideas and constructive criticism. Working with the authors at various stages has been an active team of research assistants and associates including Max Callaghan, Alieza Durana, Christopher Ellis, Sonja Kaufmann, Olga Kononykhina, Jessica Leong Cohen, Maris Moks, Joachim Rahmann, Rose Vincent, and Christopher (CJ) Yetman. Thanks are also due to Ines Andre-Schulze, Angelika Behlen, Gabriele Brühl, Magriet Cruywagen, Faye Freyschmidt, Stefanie Jost, Regine Kreitz, and Miriam Leich.

We also wish to thank the Board of the Hertie School of Governance for encouraging this Report, and for providing critical feedback and direction.

At OUP we thank Dominic Byatt for seeing the promise in this enterprise and to Olivia Wells and Carla Hodge for guiding us through.

For the Report's look we are grateful to the team of Severin Wucher and Kilian Krug at Plural in Berlin and to Emilia Birlo for the cover art work.

Finally, we are especially grateful to the Hertie Foundation for its support, and to Evonik, Stiftelsen Riksbankens Jubileumsfond, and the Berggruen Institute for providing the additional financial resources that made the Report's development and production possible.

# List of Tables, Figures, and Boxes

Table 3.1:   Comparing three families of EU decision-making
Table 5.1:   Subsample of available indicators for convergence
Figure 3.1:  Who does what in the European Semester?
Figure 5.1:  An example of convergence
Figure 5.2:  An example of convergence clubs
Figure 5.3:  Convergence in unemployment rates within the EU
Figure 5.4:  Convergence in long-term government bond yields within the EU
Figure 5.5:  Convergence in unemployment rates for countries outside the EU
Figure 5.6:  Convergence in unemployment rates, original eurozone vs. other EU countries
Figure 5.7:  Convergence in bond yields, original eurozone vs. other EU countries
Figure 5.8:  Unemployment rates over time for original eurozone member countries
Figure 5.9:  Bond yields over time for the original eurozone countries
Figure 5.10: Convergence in trust in the European Parliament
Figure 5.11: Convergence in trust in national parliaments
Figure 5.12: Convergence in trust in the European Parliament, original eurozone countries vs. other EU countries
Figure 5.13: Convergence in trust in national parliaments, original eurozone countries vs. other EU countries
Figure 5.14: Trust in the European Parliament over time for the 12 original eurozone countries
Figure 5.15: The association between unemployment rates and trust in the EU (2004-2013)
Figure 5.16: The association between unemployment rates and trust in national governments (2004-2013)
Figure 5.17: Unemployment rates and trust in the EU, by country grouping, pre-crisis (2004-2008) vs. crisis (2009-2013)
Figure 5.18: Unemployment rates and trust in national governments, by country grouping, pre-crisis (2004-2008) vs. crisis (2009-2013)

Box 1.1:  The EMU and the Eurozone
Box 2.1:  Optimum Currency Areas
Box 2.2:  Heterogeneities in the EMU
Box 3.1:  EU Institutions
Box 3.2:  Competences of the European Union

# List of Acronyms

| | |
|---|---|
| BRRD | Bank Recovery and Resolution Directive |
| CFSP | Common foreign and security policy |
| CJEU | Court of Justice of the European Union |
| EC | European Commission |
| ECB | European Central Bank |
| ECJ | European Court of Justice |
| Ecofin | Economic and Financial Affairs Council |
| ESCB | European System of Central Banks |
| EDP | Excessive Deficit Procedure |
| EEC | European Economic Community |
| EFSF | European Financial Stability Facility |
| EFSM | European Financial Stabilisation Mechanism |
| EGC | European General Court |
| EMU | economic and monetary union |
| EP | European Parliament |
| ESM | European Stability Mechanism |
| ESRB | European Systemic Risk Board |
| EU | European Union |
| GDP | gross domestic product |
| IMF | International Monetary Fund |
| MEP | Member of European Parliament |
| MIP | Macroeconomic Imbalance Procedure |
| MoU | Memorandum of Understanding |
| MTO | Medium-term budgetary objective |
| NPSJC | Network of President of the Supreme Judicial Courts of the EU |
| OMC | Open Method of Coordination |
| OMT | Outright Monetary Transactions |
| SGP | Stability and Growth Pact |
| SSM | Single Supervisory Mechanism |
| TEU | Treaty on the European Union |
| TINA | 'There is no alternative' |
| TFEU | Treaty on the Functioning of the European Union |
| TSCG | Treaty on Stability, Coordination and Governance |

# I. Introduction
## Exploratory Governance in the Euro Crisis

MARK DAWSON, HENRIK ENDERLEIN, *and* CHRISTIAN JOERGES

Is the euro crisis over? Certainly, sky-rocketing bond yields–one of the main drivers of market panic–have by now receded to pre-crisis levels, even in some of the countries worst affected by turmoil in the eurozone. Also, few people today believe that the euro is still threatened in its very existence, and instead of the frequent changes to the institutional and legal framework seen during the height of the crisis (2010-2012), there is now an astonishing silence surrounding questions related to the functioning of the economic and monetary union (EMU). With major reforms to banking supervision and resolution either in operation or nearing completion, there is seemingly little appetite for a major move towards greater political integration in the European Union (EU).

In spite of this relative calm, even a cursory look at Europe's economy and society in early 2015 reveals a storm raging below. Unemployment remains stubbornly high, even in states where labour costs have decreased significantly. Youth unemployment in particular exceeds 50 per cent in Spain and remains over 40 per cent in Greece and Italy. Levels of popular trust both in national governments and in EU institutions continue to plumb new depths. In 2005, several years before the crisis, some 57 per cent of the EU population reported trust in the EU; by 2013, the proportion had declined to 42 per cent. Similarly, trust in national governments fell from nearly 40 per cent in 2005 to 31 per cent in 2013. The early 2015 elections in Greece that brought in an anti-austerity programme government attest to remaining discontent and uncertainty. At the same time, economic recovery seems to be halting, with institutions like the International Monetary Fund (IMF) warning of the possibility of a lost decade of low growth and declining living standards (Lagarde 2011). In short, the crisis is not yet over.

Where does Europe go from here? Two things seem certain. One is that perceptions of the 'end of the crisis' may foster dangerous complacency. As

> *Pretending that the EU may simply 'muddle through' without further reform runs the risk of deferring existing risks to the next generation.*

the contributions to this Report will evidence, the present construction of the eurozone is fraught with risk, from its failure to deal adequately with economic and structural differences between member states to its inability to secure popular support and appropriate channels of political and legal control of EU-level decisions. Pretending that the EU may simply 'muddle through' its current predicament without further economic, institutional, and political reform runs the risk of deferring existing risks to the next generation.

A second certainty, however, is that reform carries a host of dangers of its own. Just as the creation of new institutions, such as for lending arrangements between EU states, have generated unexpected problems, so too will future innovations in EU governance give rise to multiple uncertainties in outcomes as well as in legal and political challenges to the implementation process. In simple terms, an EU moving towards greater fiscal and economic integration is engaging in an unparalleled experiment, lacking obvious historical or territorial precedents and with each reform fraught with contestation, risk, and uncertainty. Times are exciting but also precarious.

The purpose of *The Governance Report 2015* is to consider how EU governance has evolved since the onset of the eurozone crisis and to contemplate some of the options for the Union's economic, political, and legal future.

## How Do We Get It Right?

One key characteristic of the economic and monetary union–which became law when EU member states adopted the Maastricht Treaty– is its unprecedented set-up. The decision to bring together a dozen or more national economies within a single monetary space and with a single central bank setting a single interest rate is entirely unique. There was and still is neither a blueprint nor historical experience on which the institutional framework can be based. Policy-making thus needs to derive its orientation from one of three unreliable sources: (i) a rich but hotly debated theoretical corpus (mainly from economics), with little to no guarantee that resulting policy recommendations will produce the predicted effects; (ii) an extensive set of historical cases (for example, from fixed exchange rate regimes) that are so fundamentally different from the monetary union set-up that it will always be questionable as to what extent useful lessons can be drawn; or (iii) a very poor, almost inexistent set of monetary unions that are not at the same time fiscal federations (one of the few examples is the East Caribbean Currency Union of eight small island countries).

From a governance perspective, the lack of a blueprint makes studying the EMU incredibly fascinating, especially if looked at from an interdisciplinary angle. While economics has a tendency to rely on mechanistic theoretical assumptions and therefore risks overlooking the uniqueness of the case,

*Box 1.1* **The EMU and the Eurozone**

Although the economic and monetary union (EMU) applies to all European Union member states, only 19 have reached the third stage of integration: use of the euro as an official currency and inclusion in the eurozone (also known as the euro area). All EU member states are expected to join the euro in the future and committed to this aim when joining the EU. Three countries, however, form an exception. The UK and Denmark chose to opt out of the euro: They may join the eurozone in the future but are not obliged to do so. Sweden is not part of the Exchange Rate Mechanism, which is a necessary prerequisite for joining the euro, but is obliged to become part of the eurozone in the future.

**The Eurozone**
As of 1 January 2015, 19 of the 28 member states of the EU have adopted the euro as their currency and thereby form the eurozone. These countries share a common currency and coordinate their fiscal and economic policies. Eurozone members include: Austria, Belgium, Cyprus, Estonia, Finland, France, Germany, Greece, Ireland, Italy, Latvia, Lithuania, Luxembourg, Malta, Netherlands, Portugal, Slovakia, Slovenia, and Spain. Just before Ecofin Council meetings, finance ministers from eurozone countries meet separately in the so-called Eurogroup to discuss matters relating to the euro.

The common currency was achieved in three stages, as recommended by the Delors Report:

*Stage 1 (1990–1994):*
This stage focused on completing the internal market and laying the institutional foundations for the broader EMU. By the start of the second stage, barriers to the free movement of capital were eliminated.

*Stage 2 (1994–1999):*
On 1 January 1994, the European Monetary Institute—the European Central Bank (ECB)'s forerunner—was established. This stage emphasised technical preparation and further harmonisation of member states' economic policies.

*Stage 3 (1999 onwards):*
The introduction of the euro and the fixing of conversion rates marked the final stage establishing the eurozone. Eleven countries began using the euro as 'book money' on 1 January 1999. Greece joined in 2001, and on 1 January 2002, the first coins and bank notes were circulated.

See:
*http://ec.europa.eu/economy_finance/ euro/adoption/euro_area/ index_en.htm (2014)*
*https://www.ecb.europa.eu/ecb/ educational/facts/euint/html/ ei_004.en.html*

the legal discipline is based on a set of generalisable rules and principles from which the uniqueness of the case would be normatively assessed. Political science, finally, focuses on the interest configurations of the actors involved and how those interests are aggregated within an evolving context of institutions as the set of norms, rules, and principles shaping their interaction.

During the height of the eurozone crisis, the lack of orientation of policy actors quickly became a fact of life. While economists proposed policy solutions on a nearly daily basis and ranging from one extreme (total eurozone break-up) to the other (full debt mutualisation) with literally hundreds of intermediate options, the legal debate focused on what was allowed under EU treaty and national constitutional rules, in particular in Germany. Any actual resulting policy changes can be described as mere 'quick fixes' (Quaglia 2013) generally derived from ad hoc decision-taking under considerable time pressure and often justified by the principle of 'there is no alternative' (TINA), which was even logically wrong, given the multitude of different policy alternatives under discussion. As decisions were by definition contestable, policy-makers attempted to justify them as the only viable solutions, claiming that they knew exactly what they were doing. It will be the role of future historians to explain why and how those crisis measures were decided upon, but what is most important from our perspective are the questions of how to move on and how to get it right in the future.

If the study of governance is the study of collective decision-taking, then the question of how the eurozone will evolve in the next decade is a key governance question that deserves our attention. How can policy actors get it right if there is little to no guidance on what to do? What would be the pre-conditions for successful decision-taking? How can success be defined?

## Exploratory Governance

We suggest that the best approach for thinking about highly salient, highly contestable, and highly risky policy choices under extreme uncertainty is the concept of 'exploratory governance', which we define as ad hoc and stepwise policy-making under uncertainty with an aim of avoiding mistakes. This concept derives from a highly functional perspective of policy-making: New institutions are created to solve problems arising from within existing institutional frameworks. But in contrast to the traditional functionalist perspective of institutional change, exploratory governance puts a stronger emphasis on the totally unknown character of any newly adopted frameworks.

The EMU is a telling example: The single currency was created in response to the need for a credible fixing of exchange rates in order to allow the single market to function properly. The euro was a policy innovation that derived from dissatisfaction with the previous, ill-functioning system of fixed exchange rates in Europe. No policy actor knew at the time of the EMU's creation what the real consequences of the single currency would be, but the creation went on, based on a tightly defined set of rules and coupled with the plan to make it work. Many theorists have criticised the creation of the euro as 'incomplete' or 'ill-designed' (Eichengreen 2012), whereas others, in particular policy-makers, expressed their satisfaction and trust in the new system.

When the eurozone crisis hit, a debate started on whether the original system had lacked certain features and thus been flawed from the very start, or policy actors had violated the rules and thus destroyed a system that would have functioned properly had the existing rules been respected. Those two views then broadly converged in the perspective that the EMU was 'incomplete'– either because it lacked important features or because it had allowed violations of key rules. During the crisis, the debate on what to do was largely informed by those differences in perspective. Decisions taken were thus derived from 'exploration'–assessing the policy context, addressing immediate policy challenges, and coping with both short-term time constraints and uncertainty. If the EMU was the result of exploratory governance responding to the functional need to complete the single market, policy measures during the crisis have been the result of exploratory governance responding to the need to keep the euro alive. What lies ahead of us is yet another round of exploratory governance to complete a 'genuine' EMU as proposed by the Report of the Four Presidents of 2012 (van Rompuy et al. 2012) and a multitude of other proposals.

> *'Exploratory governance' is ad hoc and stepwise policy-making under uncertainty with an aim of avoiding mistakes.*

Many straightforward challenges arise in the context of a process of exploratory governance. First, initial proposals to adopt innovative governance structures are likely to be met with fierce opposition due to their untested character. Second, the adoption phase of new governance structures will generally be based on a strong analytical projection of the 'beneficial effects' of the innovation. Third, new governance structures have to be reconciled with existing constitutional and legitimacy commitments. Exploratory governance shares certain features in common with another framework often used to explain innovation in EU governance: democratic experimentalism (Sabel and Zeitlin 2008, 2012). However, while experimentalism is based on the idea of deliberation and bottom-up participation as a means of compensating for gaps in transnational democracy, new forms of EU governance have often been adopted without significant reflection on their accountability implications. For example, EU ambitions in the fiscal field have not been accompanied, for largely political reasons, with extensive changes in the EU's treaty structure (see Appendix for brief descriptions of the main EU treaties). Exploratory governance may face a contested gap between what is constitutionally permitted and new EU-level tasks.

Fourth, there is a high likelihood of unintended effects after the introduction of a governance innovation or, more generally, mismatches between the projected and observed effects. Fifth and finally, the nature and magnitude of the unintended effects will play a significant role in determining whether the new governance structures will be discontinued in favour of the old governance structures, will remain in place, or will remain in place but undergo significant changes, such as bringing in new elements of exploratory governance. As a process of exploratory governance is generally based on the motives of problem-solving and avoiding error, determining which of the three scenarios (discontinue, continue, or amend) will be most likely requires a comparison of the costs of going back to the initial policy problems with the costs of continuing the chosen path and the costs of further governance exploration. Obviously, the choice will be strongly linked to the perspective from which the scenario itself is derived: An economist would likely take a different stance compared to a legal scholar, a sociologist, a political analyst, or a philosopher.

# An Interdisciplinary Perspective

In this Report, we bring together three different perspectives in order to develop a consistent approach towards exploratory governance of the EMU. By combining different disciplinary perspectives, this Report aims to go beyond much of the existing work by exploring changes in EU governance through three distinct stages, each with a significant bearing on the viability of the others. Chapter 2 summarises the main considerations from the discipline of economics, outlining the main 'knowns' and 'known unknowns' in the debate on the future of the EMU. The chapter's key objective is to assess the main functional needs for the future development of the EMU that would allow the single currency to function properly. Chapter 3 then uses the lenses of law and political science to consider how new functional demands have been reconciled with the EU's existing legal and institutional structures. The key objective is to explore the institutional limitations that have shaped and altered EU decision-making since the onset of the crisis, creating in its wake severe challenges in rendering decisions under EU economic governance legally and politically accountable. Chapter 4 focuses on the law-politics relationship and its importance for the legitimacy of European rule. It argues that the reliance on law, which characterised the formative period of the integration project and which contributed to the precarious construction of the EMU, has to be replaced by a reconfiguration in which democratic political processes are structured by procedural prescriptions and safeguards, not by substantive rules or administrative decision-making.

## Getting the economics right: What is required to complete the economic and monetary union?

If the root cause of the eurozone crisis was the contradiction between a supranational currency and nation state-based economic policies, then the right exercise in the discipline of economics today should be to conduct an assessment of the steps towards further integration that are indispensable for the functioning of the EMU. The basic principle of this exercise could be 'as much additional integration as required for the functioning of the eurozone, but as little as possible'. However, there is no consensus on how that principle should be implemented.

During the first 15 years of its existence, the eurozone has been characterised by high structural heterogeneities between countries, high inflation differentials, the absence of optimum currency area criteria, and the absence of functional equivalents (such as a common budget, common taxes, or automatic cyclical stabilisers such as a common unemployment insurance or a cyclical shock insurance). At the same time, there are many reasons to believe that the structural features of many eurozone economies put an efficiency cost on domestic economies and the eurozone as a whole.

Against this background, three challenges need to be taken up in parallel:

- Structural convergence needs to be built between countries to allow for better functioning of the single currency, in particular since it would provide a better monetary policy transmission mechanism and an enhanced price transmission (or real exchange rate effect).
- For the same reasons, the single market needs to be completed to end a situation in which economic developments are to a very large extent shaped by domestic and not eurozone factors.
- Structural reforms in domestic economies need to continue to allow for an increase of potential growth and high employment rates.

Even if the assessment on overall reform needs might be quite straightforward, the exact content and degree of structural reforms to reach an optimal level of convergence and enhance growth are the subjects of considerable debate.

Different reports and studies come to different results on these questions (cf. Four Presidents' Report, Blueprint by the Commission (European Commission 2012), Report of the 'Tommaso Padoa-Schioppa Group'). The report of the Padoa-Schioppa Group (Enderlein et al. 2012) for example describes a combination of key elements that would complete the EMU while preserving a high degree of national policy-making autonomy. The 'sui generis fiscal federalism' that it proposes includes a deepening of the single market, a cyclical shock insurance fund, the equivalent of a European Monetary Fund, and the completion of the banking union.

Such lists are just illustrations of what might constitute the right degree of further integration for allowing the eurozone to work more effectively. The debate needs to be about which elements are essential. Some observers believe that the current state of integration with banking union in place is already sufficient. Others propose even more elements than are put forward here, including a much larger EU budget, a full-fledged eurozone fiscal capacity, EU taxation, and a fully developed hierarchical model of fiscal federalism.

Depending on the answers to the questions above, there are different legal and political implications. It is often unclear which proposals would require treaty change–and if so, then which variant in the large array of possible forms of treaty changes and treaty change procedures. It is also often unclear how new elements could be anchored in appropriate democratic control mechanisms in order to ensure their legitimacy. The question of possible participation by national parliaments is often raised in that respect. Answering these questions is the purpose of the next two chapters of this Report.

## New institutional arrangements, new challenges

It is clear that the EU that has taken shape since the eurozone crisis began has heightened economic and political ambitions. The EU has moved from a limited project focused on the establishment of a transnational market to a wide-ranging institution that reaches into almost every area of national policy. What do these heightened ambitions mean for the institutional, political, and legal structures through which EU policy-making is conducted?

Answering this question is the focus of the third chapter of this Report. As the chapter will argue, the radical increase in the EU's tasks brought about by the crisis has transformed EU governance, leading not only to the establishment of new institutions (for novel tasks such as banking supervision and lending) but also to a shift towards a new model of delivering EU policy. While previous EU decision-making tended to be agreed upon either through the supranational 'Community method' or through intergovernmental agreements controlled and implemented by national governments, economic governance after the onset of the crisis has tended to blend these two decision-making types in novel ways.

*The increase in the EU's tasks has transformed EU governance, leading to a shift towards a new model of delivering policy.*

The third chapter therefore introduces the idea of a 'coordinative method' of EU decision-making as an ideal type within which to understand these changes. Drawn from the Open Method of Coordination (OMC) established in the field of social policy in the late 1990s, the coordinative method represents an attempt to retain national control of key EU-level decisions, channelling the decision-making process through intergovernmental bodies such as the European Council and Eurogroup. It combines intergovernmental decision-making, however, with heightened EU capacity to intervene in and supervise national policy-making. A key example is the newly established European Semester, the strategic goals for which are set by the European Council, but which also allows an unprecedented degree of supranational intervention in the setting and coordination of national budgets. The coordinative method can be understood as an attempt to centralise or create 'more Europe' and, at the same time, maintain national control over decisions of strategic importance. Finally, the coordinative method envisages a fragmentation of obligations between states, with states subject to heightened obligations and supervision depending on their budgetary position. In simple terms, under this method, balanced budget states retain greater levels of sovereignty under the new EU economic governance than their more debt-laden neighbours.

The purpose of introducing the coordinative method as an 'ideal type' is both to understand changes in EU governance and to unpack the dilemmas these changes have brought. The primary dilemma is one of securing appropriate avenues of political and legal accountability under the coordinative method. Whereas previous models of EU decision-making sought to secure political and legal accountability–either supranationally through institutions like the European Parliament or nationally through the ability of national parliaments and judiciaries to scrutinise EU-level decisions–the coordinative method may make both political and legal review of EU-level decisions more difficult.

At the political level, this difficulty concerns the danger of marginalising the traditional role of parliaments in scrutinising budgetary decisions. At the national level, the European Semester both increases the level of supranational control over national budgetary processes and provides a heavily compressed timetable within which national parliaments can hold their executive's spending decisions to account. At the supranational level, meanwhile, the coordinative method has been a bastion of executive control, with the European Parliament given little say in the adoption of key EU-level decisions, either over general EU fiscal policy or for the adoption of recommendations addressed to specific states.

Similar problems present themselves at the legal level. Nationally, strong constitutional courts like the German *Bundesverfassungsgericht* have defended the prerogatives of the German parliament by insisting upon strict conditionality for loan assistance to southern European debtors. In the very act of doing so, however, they may have limited the ability of other constitutional courts to defend rights to equality, social assistance, and employment as guaranteed under national constitutions. Supranationally meanwhile, the coordinative method is often elaborated through 'soft law' or vague, indeterminate economic benchmarks that are unamenable to judicial review. Just as parliamentary scrutiny of EU governance has become more difficult, avenues for legal control of EU economic governance have also become increasingly scarce.

The third chapter concludes with some recommendations on closing EU governance's new 'accountability gap' and focuses on strengthening the dialogue between European and national courts and parliaments, easing coordination problems between eurozone and non-eurozone states, and re-engaging the European Parliament in the economic governance of the EU. Securing appropriate links between new EU tasks and general political processes occurring at the national and transnational levels will be a key task for EU decision-makers in the decade to come. This legitimacy dimension of new forms of EU governance is the key concern of the next chapter of the Report.

## Regaining legitimacy

The fourth chapter then addresses the legitimacy of the European project in jurisprudential perspectives. The focus on law is not accidental: As Walter Hallstein, the first President of the European Commission wrote, the Community is a creation of law, a source of law, and a legal order (Hallstein 1979: 3). 'Integration through law' was to become the trademark of the European project in its formative phase, although the original understanding of the functions of law was of course to be modified.

From early on, the European Economic Community (EEC) was understood as in need of constant adaptation in respect to the integration project. Among the most significant transformations were the new regulatory tasks that had to be addressed since the late 1980s in the course of the completion of the internal market and after the turn to governance initiated by the Commission in 2001. As integration deepened, the functions of law had to be redefined. After the widening of EU competences and the growth of EU governance, a deliberate constitutionalisation of European law was supposed to ensure the law's legitimacy-mediating functions. Though the Draft Constitutional Treaty was rejected, the debate on EU constitutionalisation did not and could not come to a standstill. Responses to the legitimacy requirement must already address the integration process so that it 'deserves recognition' (Habermas 2001). Chapter 4 seeks to capture the functions of an exploratory type of EU governance and at the same time to develop a legal framing of these functions. The challenges, however, are considerable.

The erosion of the legitimacy of the original 'integration through law' project did not occur out of the blue in the eurozone crisis, but has roots that reach back to the design of the integration project. That legitimacy was derived primarily from Europe's break with a bellicose past, but the integration project understandably did not address the political dimensions of the economy. Chapter 4 starts with a reconstruction of the two most important answers that were provided by the jurisprudence of the European Court of Justice and the concept of economic constitutionalism borne from the ordo-liberal school of thought and defended by influential German officials. It proceeds to the institutionalisation of economic rationality under the Delors Commission's internal market programme and then argues that the project of economic governance by rules ended de facto with the establishment of the EMU, which is characterised as a conceptually incoherent compromise with very limited regulatory potential. The socioeconomic diversity of eurozone members and their fiscal and economic policies caused tensions that could not be sustainably resolved by the eurozone's monetary policy and weak coordination powers over fiscal policy. Equally corrosive was the 'second pillar' of the post-war consensus on legitimate governance, namely the promise of social justice institutionalised by EU member states in a variety of welfare regimes. That legacy was confirmed through the commitment to a 'highly competitive social market economy' in Article 3(3) TEU but not supported by robust legislative or regulatory competences. The Maastricht Treaty did not consummate the project of integration through law but contributed instead to its erosion.

The chapter next analyses economic governance as reconfigured since 2010. When measured against the inherited yardstick of democratic constitutionalism, Europe's crisis management is deplorable. Economic stability was preserved only in the northern member states while the southern periphery experienced economic instability and exposure to austerity politics. However, Europe's crisis management is not criticised as a deliberate assault on the premises of the European project, but is rather understood as a response to emergencies. These responses have to remain transitory, however. If the EU were to merely normalise its recently adopted policies, the legitimacy of the integration project would remain precarious. The effort to overcome the present economic and social crises will have to consider the reasons for the non-convergence of economic and social conditions in the EU. In view of the resistance of that diversity, it is submitted that EU integration politics should cease to insist on ever more uniformity and instead focus on compatibility, hence moving towards the 'united in diversity' vision of the Draft Constitutional Treaty. That move could correct the main flaw of the integration through law agenda. It should be complemented by a reconfiguration of the law-politics relationship in which law would help to civilise contentions, stabilise constitutional accomplishments, and give voice to democratically legitimated actors, in particular the EP and national parliaments. In the process, the design and objectives of structural reforms should be reconsidered, and command-and-control practices be replaced by projects of cooperative problem-solving. Law could further contribute to the strengthening of Europe's legitimacy by a renewed emphasis on the protection of human and social rights through national constitutional courts.

> *If the EU were to merely normalise its recently adopted policies, the legitimacy of the integration project would remain precarious.*

## Governance Indicators

To these three perspectives we add a fourth that seeks to depict selected key trends in Europe in order to inform policy analysis and action. As with previous editions of *The Governance Report*, this year's team assembled a broad set of variables related to the focal topic: namely, the economic and legitimacy challenges facing the EU. Chapter 5, then, presents a sampling of the results of analyses of the extent of convergence (or divergence) of EU member states over time in terms of key economic and public opinion indicators. The analysis shows signs of convergence among EU member states in, for example, unemployment rates and long-term government bond yields until the financial crisis began, followed by increasing divergence since then. Closer examination then reveals that the divergence in economic outcomes was driven largely by eurozone member states and, among the eurozone members, by five of the countries (Greece, Ireland, Italy, Portugal, and Spain) that experienced the crisis most severely.

The data tools illustrated in the chapter (and on the Report's website: www.governancereport.org) can also be used to go beyond these basic descriptive indicators to address many analytical and policy-related questions that will inevitably arise in the process of exploratory governance.

## Conclusion

A small library full of books, articles, and reports has been written about the causes of the euro crisis and the various economic, political, and legal developments in its wake. Included among these works are our own publications, as well as a chapter on the challenges of financial and fiscal governance in the first edition of *The Governance Report* (Clark et al. 2013). The ambition of our *Report* is not to provide 'the' solution to the complex problem constellation that the euro crisis has generated. Indeed, we do not always agree entirely with each other's diagnoses or recommendations. What we want to document, however, is the potential for economic analyses, legal analyses, and jurisprudential deliberations to join forces in an interdisciplinary effort to cope with the contingencies of an unsettled situation and to explore avenues out of Europe's unsustainable present dilemmas.

Exploratory governance is not a recipe that will guide us into a secure future. Given the uncertainty of any rescue operation, exploratory governance is conceptualised rather as a search process. Neither economic functionalism, nor the EU's institutional structure, nor law can be expected to pre-programme this search. EU law and policy-making should not shy away from addressing the conflicts generated by the crisis but should rather provide fora for contestation among EU citizens, political actors, and society.

# II. The Euro as a Showcase for Exploratory Governance
## Why There Are No Simple Answers

Henrik Enderlein

## Introduction

Economic and monetary union in Europe is the first major attempt in modern history to combine a supranational monetary order with a large number of national political orders. This set-up, which at first sight starkly contradicts the traditional nation-state logic of overlapping political and economic authorities, has come under massive criticism in recent years–especially in the context of the recent eurozone crisis–due to its alleged inherent contradictions and governance failures.

> *Europe's economic and monetary union is precisely at the point at which a decision on how to continue this project of exploratory governance has to be taken.*

This chapter argues that the economic and monetary union (EMU) is a showcase for and key example of 'exploratory governance'. As discussed in the introduction to this Report, exploratory governance can be defined as the attempt to respond to deficiencies in governance structures by intentionally adopting innovative and thus untested governance structures intended to solve the initial deficiencies. In light of the eurozone crisis, Europe's economic and monetary union is precisely at the point at which a decision on how to continue this project of exploratory governance (discontinue, continue, or amend) has to be taken.

Timothy Garton Ash (2012) has frequently referred to monetary union in Europe as the 'bridge too far' in European integration.[1] When the eurozone crisis brought the euro to the brink of dissolution, it was seen as proof to many that Garton Ash's pessimistic statement had been right. But on what analytical basis can this statement be considered correct? Is there a certain degree of political integration that is required for an economic and monetary union to function effectively? Does there have to be a correspondence between economic, legal, and political institutions, perhaps even borders, to ensure that a common currency can work?

Answering these questions is a difficult task for scholars. There are almost no historical examples of such pronounced mismatches between political, economic, and monetary orders as there have been in the EMU since 1999. Also, there is still debate as to whether the eurozone crisis has been (i) the consequence of an inherently flawed approach to a monetary union in the absence of a political union (e.g. Feldstein 1997, 2012), (ii) the consequence of political misbehaviour of some countries not abiding by otherwise 'sound' rules (as frequently suggested by German Chancellor Angela Merkel (e.g. Merkel 2011)), (iii) the consequence of the so-called Great Recession, originating in the US and producing significant collateral damage in Europe (quite interestingly, what Garton Ash (2012) himself suggested[2]), or (iv) a combination of all of the above.

As this chapter will argue, the EMU is not a 'bridge too far' built out of the blue, but a functionally motivated, logical step in the process of European integration aimed at solving massive policy problems present at the time of its adoption. Given the lack of agreement on how to best fix the original policy problems, however, the EMU was established as a highly imperfect system, inherently unstable and continuously prone to collapse. During the height of the crisis, several quick fixes were adopted to prevent the system from collapsing, but these fixes failed to permanently stabilise the EMU. Today, the EMU is an almost perfect showcase for exploratory governance. Indeed, the economic and political costs and benefits of (i) returning to national currencies at the cost of re-encountering the initial policy problems, (ii) keeping the existing EMU system with all of its now apparent deficiencies, and (iii) further improving the system to correct its deficiencies (i.e. entering a new phase of exploratory governance) have to be compared. This chapter concludes that while there is no clear-cut answer to this cost-benefit analysis, the natural policy choice will likely be the third option: further amendments to the EMU and thus another round of exploratory governance with all of its implications.

# The EMU as a Functionally Motivated Step in the Process of European Integration

Understanding the creation of the EMU is impossible without contextualising it within the deeper functional logic of European integration. From the moment the idea of a single market for goods, services, people, and capital became the driving force behind European integration, there was a functional need to solve the economic policy trade-off between a system of fixed exchange rates and nationally oriented monetary policies, which would stabilise the national business cycles. As soon as political agreement on the single market project was reached in the course of the 1980s, the European Commission led by Jacques Delors began focusing on the question of the appropriate monetary regime to complement the single market. Thinking about economic and monetary union was only natural, given the large number of competitive currency devaluations in the 1980s that gave export advantages to some economies over others and thus, from the perspective of the European Commission, amounted to a simple but extremely challenging collective action problem.

Although the idea of a single currency for Europe had been proposed before (e.g. in the 'Werner Report' of 1969 or the 'MacDougall Report' of 1977), it only gained real policy momentum with an expert report coordinated by Tommaso Padoa-Schioppa in 1987, which later resulted in the adoption of the so-called Delors Report in April 1989, even before the fall of the Iron Curtain. The Padoa-Schioppa Report argued that the four freedoms of the single market–free movement of persons, services, goods, and capital– were incompatible with floating exchange rates and hence required a monetary union: 'The internal market programme creates both opportunities and needs for complementary action to foster macroeconomic stability and growth of the Community. As regards monetary stability, the elimination of capital controls, coupled to the requirement of exchange rate stability, means a qualitative change in the operating environment for monetary policy. It will require moving closer to unification of monetary policy' (Padoa-Schioppa et al. 1987: 3).

The functionalist logic behind the move to a monetary union was undeniable from the very beginning. In practical terms, trade integration in Europe was incompatible with foreign exchange rate competition between member states. While the European level was establishing a clear exclusive competence in the implementation of the single market and mainly in competition policy, regulatory policy, and standard setting, it could not fight against distorted competition that resulted from so-called competitive devaluations.

In analytical terms, the functional process of European integration, based on an overarching objective to prevent wars through economic exchanges in a single market, had reached its limit due to the incompatibility of the single market with a multitude of national currencies. As a result, the exploratory governance of European integration entered into a new round with the debate on the adoption of a single currency, an unprecedented policy challenge considering the large number of independent nations. The notion immediately gave rise to the follow-up question of whether a monetary union could exist in the absence of a political union. The single market-single currency-political union nexus was at the core of the exploratory governance debate on the EMU from the beginning.

France and Germany in particular had very different perspectives on

> **Box 2.1 Optimum Currency Areas**
>
> In general, the benefits of a currency union can be expected to outweigh its costs when it encompasses an economically homogenous area. Specifically, research on 'optimum currency areas' has stressed the importance of synchronised macroeconomic shocks and business cycles. Such synchronisation is supported by a high degree of economic openness, high capital and labour mobility, and high price and wage flexibility. Under ideal circumstances, a single monetary policy could be expected to be equally suitable for all members of a currency union—an idea that has been described as 'one size fits all'.
>
> Measured by these criteria, the euro area has never been an optimum currency area. Although it is closely connected by trade ties, labour mobility and price flexibility within the eurozone are low and the macroeconomic shocks experienced by its member states are significantly more idiosyncratic than in a smoothly working fiscal federation, based on a currency union, such as the United States. Contrary to initial expectations, synchronisation has not accelerated markedly since the start of the EMU.

how to pave the way towards a monetary union. To put things simply: France was in favour of introducing the single currency early on and creating what was often labelled a *gouvernement économique* but in fact would have aimed at using a politically controlled central bank to help alleviate intra-monetary union heterogeneities. Germany, on the other hand, was in favour of first pushing for stronger economic convergence in Europe and only then introducing the single currency as an endpoint. The final agreement that resulted in the signing and eventual entry into force of the Maastricht Treaty in 1993 was an inadequate compromise. The single currency was implemented early on, but no mechanisms were foreseen to foster convergence or assemble functional equivalents to what economists call the 'optimum currency area criteria' (see Box 2.1).

Although the political reasoning behind such a poor compromise is a topic for historians, the governance implications of that compromise go far beyond the narrow historical context. When the Maastricht Treaty was signed, it was clear to decision-makers that continuing with a fixed exchange rate system that lacked credibility and therefore gave rise to competitive devaluations was even less desirable than the imperfect Maastricht compromise. Much in line with our concept of exploratory governance, entering uncharted territory appeared a far better solution than continuing with a known but largely defective governance structure.

# One Size Fits None: The Dysfunctional Nature of the EMU

The unknown character of the EMU ex ante stemmed from the fact that the eurozone was clearly not an optimum currency area. This very simple assessment, pointing to the large structural and cyclical differences across eurozone countries, had very simple consequences. If growth and inflation rates in eurozone member states differed, then the single interest rate set by the European Central Bank (ECB) would further contribute to divergence, rather than to convergence.

When the euro was created, no one could deny that there were large structural heterogeneities in the EMU and especially among eurozone member countries. GDP per capita varies by a factor of one to eight across eurozone countries. Even if purchasing power parity rates are applied and the benchmark is not the comparison of the richest to the poorest country per capita, but the average per capita GDP rate of the eurozone as a whole, then still 12 out of 19 countries deviate by more than 15 per cent from the eurozone average (all data from Eurostat). The arguably larger intra-eurozone structural differences are important as they translate into very different member state policy preferences when it comes to coordination efforts.

**European Central Bank (ECB)**
The European Central Bank is an independent institution of the economic and monetary union (EMU) that administers the euro and the eurozone's monetary policy. Its main task is to maintain price stability and, consequently, preserve the purchasing power of the euro. The ECB and the national banks of all 28 EU member states constitute the European System of Central Banks (ESCB). The ECB's operational authority (the Executive Board) and its decision-making body (the Governing Council, including representatives of the national central banks of eurozone countries) administer the ESCB, which manages money supply, conducts exchange operations, manages foreign reserve assets, and ensures payment system functioning.

## The EMU and macroeconomic imbalances

Throughout the 1990s, many economic analysts had converged in their assessments that a single currency managed by a single central bank within a highly heterogeneous economic environment would unavoidably lead to instability. Rather than being 'one size fits all', the central bank would run the risk of becoming 'one size fits none', implementing, so to speak, the right monetary policy for a country that does not exist.

These macroeconomic imbalances were driven by diverging trends in economic activity in EMU countries: During the first ten years of the EMU, member states experienced substantial differences in national growth and inflation rates. If these divergences are partly attributable to different national economic policies and institutions (see Box 2.2), it is also true that the EMU itself holds part of the responsibility for the emergence of these macroeconomic imbalances. Three dynamics explain that effect.

- First, the ECB's monetary policy had pro-cyclical effects in those member states whose economic fundamentals were not in line with the eurozone average.
- Second, the EMU lacked the adjustment mechanisms that exist in other economically integrated areas to counter these divergences.
- Third, European institutions failed in their early warning mechanisms to detect and prevent imbalances and in asking member states to adopt the appropriate corrective measures.

Indeed, when a country enters a currency union, it abandons its most important device for absorbing temporary macroeconomic shocks: the possibility to conduct monetary policy in order to stabilise the domestic business cycle. While currency unions are still able to employ a common monetary policy to deal with symmetric shocks (i.e. those affecting the currency area as a whole), the absorption of asymmetric shocks (i.e. those affecting only one or several members of the union) becomes much more difficult. This was particularly true in the eurozone, due to the facts that labour mobility remained low and product markets were still only partially integrated.

The consequence was slow adjustments to asymmetric shocks in the presence of unsynchronised business cycles and a persistence of different growth rates and inflation differentials over the medium term. During the first decade of the EMU, member states such as Spain, Ireland, and Greece grew significantly faster than others, both in nominal and real terms, over practically the whole period between 1999 and 2008. This was accompanied by a persistent difference in inflation rates during the same period.

Both developments would not have been problems as such because the countries growing faster than average were those that had initially entered the EMU with lower GDP per capita figures. In this context, a catch-up process at higher growth rates could have even been considered normal. However, growth and inflation in these member states were above productivity growth, thus leading to losses in competitiveness and growing current account deficits. In a world with functioning adjustment channels, inflation in these countries would eventually have decreased. More integrated product markets would have led to a fall in foreign demand for domestically produced goods in boom countries, and an increase in foreign demand for domestically produced goods in bust countries; higher labour mobility would have put pressure on rising wages; sufficient levels of capital market-based insurance would have siphoned away funds to low-growth economies; and automatic stabilisers at the eurozone level would have led to transfers from boom to downturn economies, hence depressing demand in the former and boosting growth in the latter. But the divergences remained and heterogeneities increased even further.

Considering this background, it should be clear that the root cause of the eurozone crisis lay in the contradiction between a single supranational currency and the continuation of nation-state based economic policies (see also Chapter 4). This contradiction eventually gave rise to all of the other 'causes' of the crisis.

Indeed, adjustment channels in the EMU did not work as they should have, and member states faced the same short-term nominal interest rates set by the ECB. The high growth countries in particular benefitted from low real interest rates to finance their growing current account deficits in the markets, either through increased budget deficits (e.g. Greece) or through the accumulation of private sector debt, in particular at banks. That private

---

*Box 2.2* **Heterogeneities in the EMU**

One key lesson from the first decade of the EMU until the euro crisis started is that the eurozone is confronted with two types of economic heterogeneities: structural differences and cyclical divergences.

Structural differences reflect varied historical models and patterns of economic specialisation. They also point to the relative position in terms of wealth (e.g. GDP per capita) of a country in comparison to the eurozone average. Structural differences existed for the most part prior to the establishment of the EMU and are not the most important obstacle to the proper functioning of the single currency.

Cyclical divergences, on the other hand, are specific to the EMU. They point to the relative position of a country's business cycle in comparison to the business cycle position of the rest of the eurozone and can take different forms (e.g. inflation and growth differentials or imbalances in current account positions). If cyclical divergences are temporary, they are generally not a problem for the functioning of the single currency. If they persist, however, they can seriously hamper the functioning of the EMU.

Interestingly, these two types of heterogeneity are not correlated. In the early years of the single currency, eurozone member states fell into four broad categories: (i) countries in relatively weak structural positions compared to the eurozone average, but with strong cyclical performances (e.g. Portugal, Spain, and Greece in good years); (ii) countries in relatively weak structural positions and with weaker cyclical performances than average (e.g. Greece in its bad years); (iii) countries in relatively strong structural positions but with weak cyclical performances (e.g. Germany and Austria); and (iv) countries in strong structural positions and with strong structural performances (e.g. Ireland, the Netherlands, and Finland in their good years).

sector debt, however, became a government balance sheet problem when the financial crisis of 2008 and 2009 hit. As an overall consequence, market sentiments eventually turned against the original high-growth countries as their fiscal positions were no longer perceived as sustainable. This was a key factor in the outbreak of the eurozone crisis.

## The EMU and fiscal surveillance

There are two basic models to ensure fiscal discipline in fiscal federations. The first model is a market-based system in which sub-central units are induced by capital markets to conduct responsible fiscal policies. In such a system, the sub-central units have direct market access to finance their debts. A no-bailout clause allows the market to properly price default risk, defaults are possible, and monetisation of debt is prohibited. The second model is a hierarchical incentive or control system in which sub-central fiscal discipline is enforced by central rules and administrative procedures. As an ideal type, such a system usually has a lender of last resort that can assist the sub-central units in the case of unforeseen emergencies.

The original EMU approach, as enshrined in the Maastricht Treaty, mixed elements of both systems. The risk of debt default was expected to be controlled by two market-based elements: the Treaty's no-bailout clause in combination with a strict prohibition against monetising debt through the ECB. In addition, there was a hierarchical control procedure in the form of common fiscal discipline rules, laid out in the Excessive Deficit Procedure (EDP) within the Stability and Growth Pact (SGP).

The question of how to achieve domestically stabilising fiscal policies without creating a collective action problem based on free-riding deficit spending by national governments must take into consideration five main features:

- **Rules** vs. **discretion**: Are decisions on member states' fiscal stances assessed on objective grounds or based on subjective considerations, negotiations, and peer pressure?
- **Stick** vs. **carrot**: Is the framework based on penalties or on rewards?
- **Centralised** vs. **pooled**: Are assessments and decisions related to fiscal stances taken by a central authority that does not involve national governments (e.g. the Commission or an independent fiscal council), or do national governments assess and decide amongst themselves (e.g. in the Eurogroup, which brings together eurozone finance ministers, or the Ecofin Council, composed of finance ministers from the entire EU)?
- **Negative** vs. **positive**: Do common guidelines or rules set negatively formulated limits to fiscal stances (e.g. the Stability and Growth Pact approach: 'You are not allowed to run deficits above 3%'), or do they give

positively formulated indications (e.g. the Broad Economic Policy Guidelines approach: 'You should reach a budgetary deficit of 1% by 2004')?
- **Symmetric** vs. **asymmetric**: Do guidelines apply to both deficits and surpluses, or do they only apply to deficits?

The fiscal surveillance structure in the EMU was rule- and stick-based, pooled, negative, and asymmetric. The two key legal elements–the Excessive Deficit Procedure and the Stability and Growth Pact–emphasised common rules that set negatively formulated limits to fiscal behaviour and did not provide positively formulated guidance. Moreover, the rules only applied to deficits ('asymmetric rules') and not to deficits and surpluses ('symmetric rules').

Any common rule at the European level has to be either negative and asymmetric or positive and symmetric. It is impossible to devise a rule that limits member states' fiscal room for manoeuvre on the surplus side without being prescriptive; setting a surplus limit would not make any sense. In other words, the choice is between preserving an asymmetric, deficit-oriented framework of deficit prevention and agreeing on a positively formulated stance for member states' fiscal policies that can then be symmetric, giving guidelines on surpluses. The original EMU fiscal framework opted for an asymmetric and negative rule, which–in combination with the self-fulfilling character of the solvency crisis, elaborated on below–rendered crisis management more difficult.

With the experience of the crisis, the current EMU model looks even less coherent. The no-bailout clause remains intact from a legal perspective but has clearly lost its original power. Moreover, additional hierarchical control possibilities or direct intervention possibilities into the conduct of national fiscal policies have yet to be established. The current informal EMU system combines the worst elements of both the market-based and hierarchical approaches: It cannot successfully enforce the no-bailout rule but at the same time has not obtained the required transfer of sovereignty that would be needed in a hierarchical and incentive-based system.

**Stability and Growth Pact (SGP)**
A rule-based framework for EU member states, the Stability and Growth Pact (SGP) aims to maintain fiscal discipline within the economic and monetary union (EMU). The 'preventative arm' of the SGP, which entered into force in 1998, provides rules for establishing binding medium-term budgetary objectives (MTOs) for each EU government. Member states' plans for meeting their MTOs are monitored and assessed by the Commission. The 'corrective arm' of the SGP, which entered into force in 1999, constitutes the Excessive Deficit Procedure (EDP), an adjustment path for correcting excessive deficits (defined as greater than 3% of GDP) and public debt levels (greater than 60% of GDP). The SGP was first amended in 2005, then later strengthened with the Six Pack (December 2011) and Two Pack (May 2013) reforms. It continues to run in parallel to the more recent Fiscal Compact (January 2013).

The vulnerability of member states to self-fulfilling fiscal crises (de Grauwe 2011) was largely underestimated in the run-up to the EMU. The implicit assumption at that time was that, given the establishment of credible and effective mechanisms to ensure budgetary discipline at the national level, the risk of an EMU sovereign default would be close to zero. The crisis, however, has revealed the shortcomings of the current EMU fiscal discipline regime.

First, the failure of some eurozone member states to comply with the rules of the original Stability and Growth Pact was a root cause of fiscal misbehaviour. While it is certainly true that these episodes negatively affected the credibility of the fiscal surveillance mechanism in general and the likelihood that sanctions would be applied in particular, fiscal misbehaviour should not be seen as the starting point of the crisis. There was fiscal misbehaviour in several eurozone countries, yet some countries that had misbehaved (in particular Germany) did not run into a crisis, whereas other countries that had played by the rules (notably Spain and Ireland) experienced major difficulties. It is therefore much more likely that an institutional framework conducive to self-fulfilling solvency crises played a much more important role in the recent crisis events than the deficiencies of, or non-compliance with, the Stability and Growth Pact or the Excessive Deficit Procedure.

Second, the crisis also showed that the degree of financial integration in the EMU is such that when some member states are pushed into a bad equilibrium, other member states are also affected. As a result, strong externalities are created, making it impossible to isolate one country's financial problem from the rest of the eurozone. Due to the interdependency of the EMU's banking system and its economies, the disorderly default of any member state will likely generate strong negative effects in the European financial system and runs the risk of triggering a domino effect to other vulnerable EMU economies.

In sum, until the beginning of the crisis, little attention was paid by European decision-makers to the major macroeconomic imbalances that had been emerging in the eurozone since the early 2000s. The crisis, however, revealed that these imbalances could be a threat to the stability of the entire currency union.

Or, to use the terminology of this chapter, the unintended consequences of the newly adopted currency union had suddenly produced unforeseen costs that, in the view of many, started to outweigh the initial benefits of the monetary union. The process of exploratory governance had reached the point at which it was clear that simply continuing the project was impossible. Just as suddenly, the three main options were to discontinue the EMU, to muddle through with some quick fixes, or to fundamentally review the governance structures of the EMU.

# Exploratory Governance and the Crisis: Quick Fixes vs. Corner Solutions

When the crisis first hit Greece in late 2009, almost no one in Europe expected the isolated Greek case to generate implications for the stability of the entire eurozone project. As a consequence, the debate over the Greek debt burden was a highly emotional, even polemic one, in particular in Germany, where the public discussion quickly focused on whether the crisis country should be asked to leave the eurozone and default on its debt. Quite strikingly and after initial hesitations, the German government clearly took the position that Greece should not leave. While one of the reasons was certainly the fear that a 'Grexit' would produce uncontrollable contagion effects across the entire eurozone and damage the German banking system, the more fundamental debate focused on whether a currency union that made it possible for member countries to leave was not simply a fixed exchange rate regime in all but name.

Soon after the outbreak of the crisis in Greece, doubts about the financing capacity of several other eurozone countries emerged. From a financial market perspective, that consequence was plausible. In a currency union, the risk of default for individual member states tends to increase significantly, as individual countries no longer have the possibility to issue their debt in the common currency. A debt crisis in a currency union is functionally equivalent to what the sovereign debt literature calls a 'foreign currency debt crisis'. As a consequence, as soon as the first doubts about the repayment capacity of highly indebted eurozone countries surfaced, the dynamic became a self-fulfilling prophecy, leading quickly to interest rate levels at which the sustainability of public finance was impossible to guarantee.

What followed was a sequence of rescue operations at various levels, seeking to (i) provide emergency loans to Greece and several other EU crisis countries through an ad hoc European Financial Stability Facility (EFSF), (ii) institutionalise that loan provision within a more permanent European Stability Mechanism (ESM) connected to the EU treaties, and (iii) decrease the upward pressure on crisis countries' interest rates through sovereign debt purchases by the European Central Bank. Those rescue operations were accompanied by contractually agreed structural reform commitments from crisis countries–Memorandums of Understanding (MoUs)–that

---

**European Stability Mechanism (ESM)**
Established in October 2012, the ESM is a permanent intergovernmental organisation with the 19 eurozone countries as its shareholders. The ESM provides conditional loans to member states, purchases member state bonds, assists member states via precautionary credit lines, and directly recapitalises financial institutions. The ESM was preceded by two temporary funding programmes, the European Financial Stability Facility (EFSF) and the European Financial Stabilisation Mechanism (EFSM).

were constantly monitored by the so-called Troika, consisting of the European Commission, the ECB, and the International Monetary Fund (IMF).

The reasoning behind that sequence of rescue measures was to counter severe market reactions while ensuring that crisis countries committed to debt reductions and significant structural reforms as listed in the MoUs. The main political difficulty was finding the right balance between imposing reforms on crisis countries from 'outside' (i.e. the Troika) and offering incentives in the form of bailout funds. Notably, the crisis countries faced extensive internal political destabilisation, leading in several cases to the collapse of existing governments and the election or appointment of technocratic regimes tasked with managing the reforms (e.g. the Papademos government in Greece and the Monti government in Italy). At the same time, debates in the creditor countries (in particular Germany) on whether to provide more bailout money became increasingly difficult, both politically and legally. Showdowns between creditors and debtors became more frequent, resulting in political deadlocks driven by the unwillingness of crisis countries to engage in more politically costly reforms and the unwillingness of creditor countries to provide money under the uncertainty of no further reform efforts. Mid-2012 saw the height of the crisis, with no immediate solution in sight until August 2012, when ECB President Mario Draghi announced the creation of a programme of outright monetary transactions (OMT) intended to reduce the interest rate differential on sovereign bonds between 'core' and 'periphery' member states. The programme, which Draghi defended as motivated exclusively by monetary policy considerations to enhance the transmission mechanism of monetary policy in the eurozone, was perceived in international financial markets as a guarantee against the break-up of the eurozone.

**Outright Monetary Transactions (OMT)**
Announced in August 2012, outright monetary transactions (OMT) constitute an ECB programme in which the bank can purchase bonds issued by a euro area member state in secondary, sovereign bond markets so as to bring down borrowing costs for a country, and thereby enhance the monetary transmission mechanism. The announcement of the OMT was seen as a sign that the ECB would prevent a self-fulfilling fiscal crisis that would force a country out of the euro area. In order to activate the OMT, a member state must receive direct macroeconomic support or conditioned credit lines from the European Stability Mechanism (ESM), comply with existing conditionalities, and have complete access to private lending markets. As of February 2015, the OMT had not been activated, and signs of a planned activation are not evident. The OMT is often seen as a tool deriving its effectiveness from its announcement, rather than from implementation.

The OMT announcement is the most tangible turning point in the eurozone crisis, even within the wider context of other important measures taken in 2012. The creation of a banking union, which entered into effect in late 2013, marked an important step in the efforts to break the nexus between banks and sovereign nation states.

Overall, there seems to be a general understanding that the progress in 'completing' the EMU needs to continue. In December 2014, the conclusions of the European Council stated that 'Closer coordination of economic policies is essential to ensure the smooth functioning of the Economic and Monetary Union' (European Council 2014: 3) and invited the preparation of an 'analytical note' to be discussed in the first half of 2015. A late-2014 study by the Bertelsmann Stiftung and Jacques Delors Institut–Berlin argues that 'Europe's economic and monetary union (EMU) is not viable in the long run' (Enderlein and Fritz-Vannahme 2014: 8).

## What Are the Next Steps in the 'Exploratory Governance' of the EMU?

The eurozone crisis has not been about the euro; its origins clearly did not lie in the single currency itself (c.f. Fratzscher forthcoming). The crisis was sparked by the incapacity of both the EU and its member states to ensure the conduct of economic policies aimed at getting different national economic systems to coexist with a single currency.

Today, there are good reasons to believe that the 'old' EMU system cannot survive. If that is the case, then in the logic of exploratory governance, there are only two remaining options. One is to discontinue the entire project. The other is to continue the process of exploratory governance in order to improve the old system. Such a move forward obviously triggers the difficulty of continuing further in the direction of uncharted territory, unknown consequences, and the possibility of new unintended effects.

In other words, there are two basic trajectories that could eliminate, or even reduce, current challenges in the EMU. Either Europe returns to different currencies, which would threaten the future of the single market and, with it, the future of the common project for political integration; or Europe succeeds in bringing the different national economic systems in line so as to allow the euro to function properly as a single currency.

The second option to 'complete the euro' is often confused with some kind of blueprint for a European 'superstate' or a 'United States of Europe'. It is not clear why such a structure derived from the nation-state system of governance would be needed. Rather, what could be established is a sui generis form of fiscal federalism, which would derive from the functional deficiencies of the current common currency framework while respecting to the largest extent possible the budgetary autonomy of eurozone member countries. To put things simply, one could argue that the single currency needs as much fiscal federalism as necessary for its appropriate functioning, but no more.

The question is to what extent there can be agreement on the necessary degree of further integration. Here are two possible avenues toward generating debate around ideas that could become the foundation for further integration in the spirit of exploratory governance. The following assessments focus on current challenges to the EMU as outlined in this chapter, as well as possible solutions.

The first challenge lies in the tension between a key factor in European integration—the internal market—and the major structural differences within Europe. The single market is not compatible with fluctuating exchange rates, which would make it possible for countries to recover competitive advantage in the short term through devaluation. Thus, as argued above, the blueprint for a common currency was the practical and logical answer for the single market. Unfortunately, contrary to initial expectations, the common currency has not eliminated the economic heterogeneities that existed among its member countries. Price differences within the eurozone have increased rather than decreased. As a consequence, the key interest rates set by the European Central Bank have never actually been suited to any member state. Those interest rates have had damaging and even pro-cyclical effects that have tended, in most of the member states, to be self-reinforcing. This situation has led to excessive imbalances and cyclical divergence within the eurozone.

To meet this challenge, it is necessary first and foremost to continue to pursue the completion of the internal market. A fully integrated commercial area with extensive trade relations is likely to spark enhanced price convergence and is, therefore, an important element in the functioning of an effective common monetary policy. Not only is the service industry still rooted in the national sphere to the tune of 80 per cent, but the free movement of people across borders also encounters a number of obstacles: Pension rights, for example, are very difficult to transfer from one country to another.

In parallel with measures designed to strengthen the internal market, it might also become necessary to compensate for some of the cyclical disparity within the eurozone. Such compensation has been achieved in the United States and Germany by way of a common taxation system or a form of unemployment insurance. Advances like unemployment insurance may appear desirable to convinced pro-Europeans, but they are not the only solution. For instance, what could be proposed instead are schemes for contributing towards cyclical stabilisation in an effort to counter excessive business cycle fluctuations. In a system of this kind, countries enjoying a boom would contribute to the fund while those in a recession would benefit from it. Over the longer term, transfers would not necessarily occur in only one direction. For instance, if the system had existed over the past years, Germany would have benefited from it when its growth rate slowed at the start of the last decade, and when Ireland and Spain were both enjoying a boom, they would have contributed to the fund and prevented their national economies from later spinning out of control. Today, of course, the situation would be in reverse.

Such a system would reduce cyclical divergence within the eurozone and thus ensure that the ECB's monetary policy would become more effective (c.f. Enderlein, Guttenberg, and Spiess 2013).

The second major challenge lies in the tension between independence in the area of financial policy and coordination within a monetary union. How far does a country's national sovereignty over its own budget policy extend when all of the other member states in the currency zone will be impacted by those decisions? Would a total transfer of authority over budgetary policy-making have to be transferred to the European level?

One possible approach could be a scheme of 'federalism by exception' (Delors and Enderlein 2012). Under normal circumstances, each country would be independent in setting its budget policy in accordance with the eurozone's established rules of fiscal policy-making. However, should a country's debt get out of control, another mechanism would have to be adopted. One could suggest that in a monetary union, sovereignty ends when solvency ends (Enderlein et al. 2012). In practical terms, this would mean that when a country no longer has access to a financial market, it would gradually transfer its sovereignty in budgetary policy-making to the European level. The quid pro quo could be simple: The greater the financial dependence of a country on European financing, the deeper the transfer of sovereignty and thus the European Union's scope for intervention. One proposal could work as follows: An enhanced ESM (or a sort of European monetary fund) would be guaranteed at the Community level and would issue common bonds to finance a certain pre-agreed share of member state debt or GDP. Were that rate at 10 per cent of GDP, Germany, for instance, would still continue to finance more than 80 per cent of its public debt in the form of national bonds. Should a country no longer have access to capital market financing, however, it could obtain rapid and flexible funding through the jointly issued bonds. As counterparty, that country would have to agree to the gradual transfer of its sovereignty. In extreme cases, countries with debt levels exceeding 60 per cent of their GDP (the Maastricht rule) would be constrained to submit their budget for EU approval. A process of this kind would obviously require a strong democratic base: One could imagine parliamentary supervision of such an approval mechanism in a mixed commission comprising representatives of both the European Parliament and national parliaments.

# Conclusion

The EMU is a showcase for exploratory governance. Although it was established to fix policy problems, its implementation suffered from fundamental deficiencies and thus generated a multitude of unintended consequences. Today, the debate on whether to dismantle the EMU or keep it completely unchanged no longer seems to be the right debate. Indeed, rather than trying to answer the question of whether the costs of the current regime are lower than the costs of returning to the old regime, it seems natural that policy choices should focus on the nature of further amendments to be adopted in order to make the single currency work. Further theoretical work is needed on exploratory governance, but it might be a key feature of such a logic that, once adopted, is likely to give rise to additional rounds of exploratory governance with all its implications.

In this context and in the coming years, Europe will have to seek to demonstrate that a multi-level governance approach to conducting economic policy can work. This demonstration will in all likelihood occur through action and actual policy exploration, not only in spirit or through declarations. The chosen process will have to formulate a response to the unique challenge posed by the common monetary project: How can economic policy in the EMU be conducted in an effective way in absence of the traditional nation-state foundations? What kind of fiscal federalism can be envisaged for a Union of member nations that want to continue to preserve their domestic identities and political cultures, but at the same time continue to be interconnected on the basis of the four freedoms, which in turn imply a single currency?

In sum, an appropriate governance framework for the European Union will need to combine elements of the old nation-state environment with more innovative forms of supranational governance. Building such a framework is paramount to overcoming the trade-off between preserving strong domestic political legitimacy and solving supranational challenges, in particular economic challenges arising from the single market at the European level. What probably will need to emerge is a sui generis construct that can respond to that trade-off. Jürgen Habermas's idea of a non-state supranational democratic order *(entstaatlichtes supranationales Gemeinwesen)* could serve as the blueprint for such a new governance model (Habermas 2012: 27).

## Endnotes

1   'For today, it is precisely the forced march to unity—across the "bridge too far" of monetary union—that is threatening the very achievement it is supposed to complete' (Garton Ash 1999). After the outbreak of the crisis, Garton Ash (2012) noted: 'Europe's monetary union was a bridge too far—meaning not a bridge that should never have been crossed but a bridge that was crossed too soon, before Europe was strategically prepared to defend it.'

2   Garton Ash (2012): 'To be sure, the initial shocks that started the earthquake came from outside Europe, in the US subprime mortgage market. In this sense, the travails of the eurozone are part of a broader crisis of Western financial capitalism.'

# III. The Euro Crisis and Its Transformation of EU Law and Politics

MARK DAWSON

## Introduction

The European Union has always carried a frustratingly complex decision-making framework that reflects a series of compromises between EU institutions, member states, and a number of non-governmental and private interests. While difficult to comprehend, this political structure has been important in stabilising the Union in moments of crisis and delivering the integrated trans-national market of the EU today (Dawson and de Witte 2013). It is also, however, a structure designed for a specific era and a specific view of what the EU 'is' as an organisation. To take one example, the Community method–the traditional means of creating EU law–was based on the notion that EU legislation should be founded on a high level of consensus and should observe a strict division between EU and national powers (Dehousse 2011). The EU under this method was seen as a supranational organisation with limited tasks, encouraged to break down national barriers to trade but unable to possess the resources and steering capacity of a government or to fundamentally re-organise core elements of national policy.

> *EU decision-making and the balance of power between EU institutions have been fundamentally transformed.*

If we fast-forward to the EU taking shape following the 2014 parliamentary elections, we see fundamental shifts. The creation of new institutions such as the European Stability (or bail-out) Mechanism (ESM), as well as the increasing power of the Union to interfere in national budgets in order to safeguard the eurozone, has significantly heightened the ambitions of EU policy. The EU is no longer a limited organisation but one engaged in redistribution, both between and within states (Chalmers 2012). Little wonder then that EU decision-making and the balance of power between EU institutions have been fundamentally transformed. As highlighted in the introduction to this Report, new institutional formations

*Box 3.1* **EU Institutions**

**Council of the European Union (the Council)**

The Council of the European Union (also known as 'the Council of Ministers') is comprised of ministers from all EU member states and is an essential decision-making body in the EU. Which 'configuration' of ministers is called to Council meetings depends on the policy issue being discussed. The Council, together with the European Parliament (EP), passes European laws and adopts the EU's budget. In addition, the Council is the lead institution for decision-making on the Common Foreign and Security Policy (CFSP) and economic policy coordination, and concludes international agreements between the Union and external countries and organisations.

The Economic and Financial Affairs Council (Ecofin), the configuration of member state economic and finance ministers, handles EU economic policy, taxation issues, and financial services regulation. Ecofin also hosts special sessions with national budget ministers and the European Commissioner for financial programming and budget in order to prepare the EU's annual budget.

**Court of Justice of the European Union (CJEU)**

The Court of Justice of the European Union encompasses the whole judiciary of the EU. It comprises the Court of Justice (ECJ), the General Court (EGC), and the specialised European Union Civil Service Tribunal. The CJEU ensures that EU law is applied identically in each member state by assessing the legality of EU institutional actions, ensuring member state compliance, and ruling on the interpretation and validity of provisions contained in EU law at the request of national courts. The Court of Justice and the General Court also adjudicate in disputes between EU institutions, member states, businesses, and individuals, while the Civil Service Tribunal handles cases between civil servants and the Union.

**European Commission (EC)**

The European Commission, the EU's executive arm, currently comprises 28 Commissioners, one from each member state. In consultation with member state governments, the EC President, elected by the European Parliament (EP), nominates the Commissioners, which are then approved by the EP for a five-year term. The EC acts in the general interest of the Union with complete independence from national governments. Its main tasks are to propose legislation to the Council and EP, implement EU policies and the budget, oversee the application of European law jointly with the Court of Justice of the European Union (CJEU), and represent the European Union on the international stage in matters not relating to the Common Foreign and Security Policy.

**European Council**

The European Council, not to be confused with the Council of the European Union, comprises the heads of state or government from all member states, plus the President of the European Council and the President of the European Commission. Meeting at least four times a year, the European Council gives the EU political direction and sets its priorities in the form of consensus-based 'conclusions' which delegate issues to the Council of the European Union.

**European Parliament**

The European Parliament (EP) is an assembly of 766 representatives (as of the 2015 elections) from all 28 member states, whose number of seats are allotted based on EU population share. Members of the European Parliament (MEPs) are directly elected by EU citizens every five years. The EP's three main roles are: passing laws (a power shared with the Council); determining and monitoring the Union's budget (again a power shared with the Council); and supervising EU institutions, in particular the Commission.

*For further information, see*
*http://europa.eu/about-eu/institutions-bodies/*

are being explored that carry few historical precursors. (See Box 3.1 for an overview of the key EU institutions.)

The purpose of this chapter of *The Governance Report* is to identify this transformation by describing and analysing the state of EU governance in 2015. In doing so, this chapter will track two main questions. The first concerns how decisions in the EU emerging from the crisis are made. As the sections below will demonstrate, the crisis has led to the emergence of a new decision-making constellation: the 'coordinative method'. This method carries institutional relations and modes of legitimation distinct from previous models of EU governance. EU decision-making during the euro crisis displays paradoxical tendencies: It increasingly combines highly centralised supranational intervention, particularly in budgetary policy, with intergovernmental control of key political decisions. In short, governments have demanded 'more Europe' but not at the cost of national decision-making control, a level of control that is greater for debt-free states than for debt-ridden ones.

The second question concerns securing political and legal accountability in future EU decision-making. Whereas previous methods of EU decision-making carried distinct mechanisms to render EU decisions accountable, either legally or through parliamentary scrutiny, the institutional and decision-making framework emerging from the crisis has created a number of gaps in this accountability structure. The coordinative method tends to render obsolete traditional mechanisms of judicial review and parliamentary control without substituting new models in their place. The chapter will conclude with some suggestions as to how this accountability gap could be addressed in the future.

# Four Factors of Change in EU Decision-Making

Before identifying the current model of EU decision-making, we have to understand the factors that drive adaptation in European decision-making. While one could point to many such factors, we will focus here on four main factors of change.

1. The first of these is **functionality**. In simple terms, EU decision-making has evolved as the EU has developed new powers and tasks. The growth of regulatory agencies with specialised functions, of new institutions such as the European Central Bank (ECB), and of new office holders such as the High Representative for Foreign Affairs speaks to functional pressures that have changed the way decisions in the EU are made.
2. The second factor of change is **diversity**. Functional expansion is always mediated by limits, most often imposed by the member states, to accommodate national diversity. This carries two dimensions. Both the widening (i.e. the addition of new member states) and the deepening (i.e. the entry into sensitive and complex areas of policy) of the EU have heightened the complexity of EU decision-making. The gradual shift of decision-making in the Council from unanimity to qualified majority voting and the increasing use of national opt-outs are good examples of an EU decision-making structure evolving to both accommodate national differences and ensure that these differences do not disrupt or halt the decision-making process (Scharpf 2003).
3. The third factor of change is **effectiveness**. Decision-making methods may vary depending on the instruments used to deliver EU policy and perceptions of their utility. For policy goals requiring a rapid response or displaying a high degree of functional complexity (e.g. the ECB's decisions on monetary policy or the Commission's regulation of chemicals or food safety) decision-makers may seek to avoid cumbersome legislative processes. For action in sensitive policy areas such as cultural policy, education, or criminal justice, a higher degree of consultation may be necessary both to secure national acceptance for policies agreed trans-nationally and to ensure that member states comply domestically with these policies.
4. Finally, an important factor of change is **legitimacy**. Changes in EU decision-making have also been affected by perceptions of what type of decision-making structure can be normatively defended to citizens. Politically, the rise in the EU's powers has required greater citizen input and the parliamentarisation of EU decision-making. At the same time, legally, the development of mechanisms by which individuals and institutions can judicially review political decisions of EU institutions is also driven by the demand for a system of 'checks and balances' able to censure possible abuses of power in an EU context (Curtin 2009: 54).

*Box 3.2* **Competences of the European Union (Art. 3-6 TFEU)**

**Exclusive competences**
The EU is the only actor setting binding rules for member states in the following policy fields: customs union; monetary policy for the eurozone; common commercial policy; assurance of competition for functioning of the internal market; conservation of marine biological resources; and conclusion of international agreements.

**Shared competences**
As long as the EU has not exercised or decided to use its competences, member states may adopt binding legislation in these policy areas: internal market; social policy; economic, social, and territorial cohesion; agriculture and fisheries (except conservation of marine biological resources); environment; consumer protection; transport; trans-European networks; energy; areas of freedom, security, and justice; and public health. This restriction does not apply to the areas of research and technology, space, and humanitarian aid, where member states are able to enact their own legislation complementary to EU legislation.

**Special competences**
- Economic and employment policies: The EU coordinates these policy areas and lays out the broad framework for the member states.
- Common Foreign and Security Policy: The EU is not allowed to adopt binding legislation in this field, but has competences in all areas related to the CFSP.
- Flexibility clause: In special, highly regulated cases, the EU is able to exceed its competences as assigned in the treaties.

**Supporting competences**
With member states having the sole right to adopt binding legislation, the EU can only offer coordination or support in the following policy areas: human health; industry; culture; tourism; education, vocational training, youth, and sport; civil protection; and administrative cooperation.

*See http://europa.eu/legislation_summaries/institutional_affairs/treaties/lisbon_treaty/ai0020_en.htm*

# Two Families of EU Decision-Making

These factors of institutional evolution have often combined to drive dramatic changes in EU decision-making. Even before the emergence of significant turmoil in the eurozone, they led to the development of a 'twin-track' decision-making structure during the time of the Maastricht treaty negotiations in the early 1990s. This structure and its failings are important for understanding the nature of the EU institutions today. Two broad families of decision-making, each of which responds to these dimensions of change in different ways, embody these tracks (Fabbrini 2013).

The first of these families is the so-called Community method. The Community method has existed to some degree from the formation of the Union but has undergone significant change. Its contemporary instantiation is based on the main method for agreeing on law, the so-called Ordinary Legislative Procedure (Art. 294 Treaty on the Functioning of the EU (TFEU)), with the following dominant features:

- The Commission carries a **monopoly on initiative** and control of the legislative agenda.
- **Legislative agreement is needed** between the member states (in the form of the Council) and the European Parliament, with the former normally voting by qualified majority.
- **Decisions result in legislation,** judicially reviewable at the EU level and based on enumerated treaty-based powers, (or 'competences'; see Box 3.2). Legislative measures in areas outside the EU's powers may be judicially challenged.
- The **Commission implements EU-level measures supranationally,** either through delegating/implementing legislation or in concert with governments in agency structures. Some laws, including Directives, are implemented at the national level; their effects are safeguarded by the individual right to enforce EU obligations in front of national courts or the Commission's right to prosecute governments that fail to implement EU obligations properly.
- Binding EU measures carry **presumed supremacy over conflicting national laws.**
- **Legitimacy is output- and consensus-based** in that it relies on the delivery of functional goals that national governments could not deliver on their own, and on the high degree of consensus needed for legislation to be passed.

While it is difficult to summarise this method in a few sentences, two features seem to stand out. The first is that the Community method involves high levels of supranational control. The second is that this control is compensated by its emphasis on consensual decision-making, i.e. that different institutions (and the interests that they represent) must all agree before EU legislation can be passed. The Community method was the dominant mode of decision-making until the Maastricht Treaty in 1993 and remains dominant in many fields today, including environmental policy, the internal market, and agriculture, amongst others.

There were, however, continual challenges to this method, particularly along the diversity and legitimacy factors discussed above. To what extent, for example, could such a method be used in new areas of EU action that pertained more closely to traditional national prerogatives? During the Maastricht negotiations, national governments were faced with two new significant functional imperatives: firstly, the creation of a single currency and secondly, the need for common cooperation and capacity in the fields of defence and security in the wake of the ongoing conflict in the former Yugoslavia. These were policy fields in which national implementation structures differed radically and which spoke to core national concerns (Fink-Hooijer 1994). Member states were simply unwilling to hand over significant political control to supranational bodies in such areas.

As a result, Maastricht saw the increasing channelling of EU action into a two-tier structure underlain by two separate treaty frameworks. In the Treaty on European Union (TEU), the dominant mode of decision-making would be the intergovernmental method: a decision-making type more reminiscent of ordinary international organisations. Its main features include:

- **Agenda-setting is controlled by the member states** via the Council and European Council.
- **Agreements are made by the Council,** with the Commission and EP largely acting as observers. In foreign policy, unanimous agreement is normally required.
- **Agreements may or may not carry the form of binding law.** In foreign policy, decisions and common positions are binding for the EU and its member states; in economic governance, non-binding recommendations predominate.
- **Member states ensure that common positions are observed.** EU supervision takes place only in cases of significant non-compliance (e.g. with Maastricht's 3% public deficit criteria).
- **Judicial review operates primarily at the national level** once EU measures have been domestically implemented. EU-level judicial review is precluded, with limited exceptions.
- **Policies are legitimated based on output,** that is, on the benefits of coordination in these fields and on the democratic legitimacy of the national governments, accountable for their decisions at the domestic level, agreeing to them.

In contrast to the Community method's high level of supranational control and keenness to include actors such as the European Parliament and Commission in decision-making, the intergovernmental method focuses strongly on intergovernmental monopolies of both the design and the implementation of EU policies.

The intergovernmental method faced many challenges of its own. Here, the main challenges related to the effectiveness and legitimacy factors. In terms of effectiveness, the difficulty was in ensuring national implementation of EU policies and thereby guarding against free-riding behaviour. In the context of the eurozone, for example, the Maastricht Treaty's limits on debts and deficits were frequently flouted as a consequence of alliances between states keen to avoid debilitating financial penalties (Schelkle 2007). In terms of legitimacy, the fragmentation of the treaty structure created in Maastricht and the lack of availability of judicial review or parliamentary control led to demands for the consolidation and simplification of decision-making (cf. the 2001 Laeken declaration).

While these demands were partially met by the Lisbon Treaty, the twin-track structure, including the presence of two separate EU treaties, remained. Differentiation in EU policy-making was here to stay, with some issue areas channelled through the intergovernmental method and others, including justice and home affairs, returned to the Community method. As we will see, the search for new decision-making models is a trend that the euro crisis has considerably accelerated.

## The Crisis and Its Legacy

How has the crisis altered the balance between these two methods or even introduced a third track? The crisis has produced pressures along each of the aforementioned 'factors of change' in EU decision-making.

1. The primary strain is **functional** (cf. Chapter 2). By requiring intervention in core areas of national fiscal and social policy, EU decision-making since the onset of the crisis carries a totalising character quite different from the Maastricht settlement. Decision-making must change to reflect EU intervention in core state powers, which carry significant re-distributive consequences between European states (Genschel and Jachtenfuchs 2013). As with previous changes, the development of new EU functions such as banking supervision or debt assistance has driven the demand for new institutions and voting rules.
2. The second strain relates to **diversity**. If the Maastricht Treaty was designed to accommodate divergent preferences and institutional

structures between member states in fiscal and security policy, new EU competences in the economic domain suggest a far greater willingness to harmonise national rules. This deepening, however, poses the same challenge as before: How can it be accommodated without provoking significant national disagreement? Diversity and the creep of the EU into sensitive policy domains drive the demand for intergovernmental control. Yet, as will be explored below, the need for effective coordination drives an opposite demand for centralisation. This diversity paradox is the demand to provide a system of decision-making that is nationally controlled while avoiding the high numbers of veto players that made the Maastricht regime of economic governance so precarious.

3. Thirdly, **effectiveness** is also a key driver of change. Both the Community method and intergovernmental method face significant effectiveness challenges when applied to economic governance. While the Community method involves a cumbersome, rules-based decision-making process, effective economic governance may require detailed and rapid intervention in national economic policies–a type of intervention unsuited to traditional hierarchical regulation (Armstrong 2013). In terms of the intergovernmental method, how can we secure national compliance on the basis of largely voluntary goals, particularly when meeting such goals may come at a significant financial or political cost? The consensual mode of decision-making of the Community method may be too cumbersome, just as the multilateralism of the intergovernmental method may be too prone to political manipulation.

4. The final factor of change during the crisis has been related to **legitimacy** (cf. Chapter 4). Previous models of EU legitimation seem to fail when applied to the demands of a renewed eurozone. Output legitimacy under the Community method was based on the idea that all states could agree on the desired output of integration. The shift of EU regulation into core state powers, however, questions that assumption (Majone 2012: 7-12). In coordinating national economies, what should be the end goal: fiscal discipline, economic growth, sustainable economic development, social equality, or other objectives? The intergovernmental method also faces challenges. The dominance of intergovernmental bodies in this method leaves out a number of important interests, in particular the voices of EU citizens. Finally, this method does a poor job of accounting for disparities of power between member states. As the crisis quickly illustrated, the agendas of institutions such as the European Council are easily dominated by larger and better resourced member states, with the preferences of smaller states, particularly those not in the eurozone, frequently sidelined during the crisis period (Dawson and de Witte 2013: 828-36).

In simple terms, the two prior methods' weaknesses in terms of functionality, diversity, effectiveness, and legitimacy when tackling the challenges of the crisis have led, in keeping with the framework of exploratory governance, to a search for new decision-making constellations. As will be argued below, the euro crisis has seen the development of a coordinative method that combines yet also moves beyond both of these previous models.

## The Coordinative Method: A Third Family of Decision-Making?

The coordinative method originated prior to the euro crisis. In the late 1990s, the demand from a wave of newly elected centre-left governments for coordinated EU action in the social domain led to the establishment of the Open Method of Coordination (OMC): a multi-lateral surveillance process for the coordination of social and employment policies. From 2000, the OMC was further generalised, forming the centrepiece of the Lisbon Strategy, a framework to improve the EU's economic competitiveness.

The attraction of the OMC in the 1990s was due to certain features of its design, features also apparent in current models of economic governance. Primarily, the OMC was designed as a process of soft law that could operate in areas such as fiscal and social policy where the EU had limited powers. As an instrument of soft law, it was chiefly for governments to design the OMC's overall norms. At the same time, EU institutions were to play an important role in monitoring national compliance. Reluctant to cede competences and control to the EU level, yet still requiring centralised supervision and coordination of policy, the OMC was seen by national governments as the 'best of both worlds' or as a constitutional compromise between supranational and national visions (Zeitlin 2005).

Although it seemed for many years that 2000 would be the OMC's high-water mark, the Union's move to strengthen economic governance from 2010 onwards involved significant reliance on this method, including its expansion into new areas. Before examining why, it may be useful to outline the coordinative method's main features. The modified Excessive Deficit Procedure (EDP) and newly created Macroeconomic Imbalances Procedure (MIP) illustrate well some of the coordinative method's central elements. These two procedures form part of the larger European Semester, a yearly cycle of economic coordination that brings together a number of EU coordination processes (see Figure 3.1). Features of the coordinative method include the following:

*Figure 3.1* **Who does what in the European Semester?**

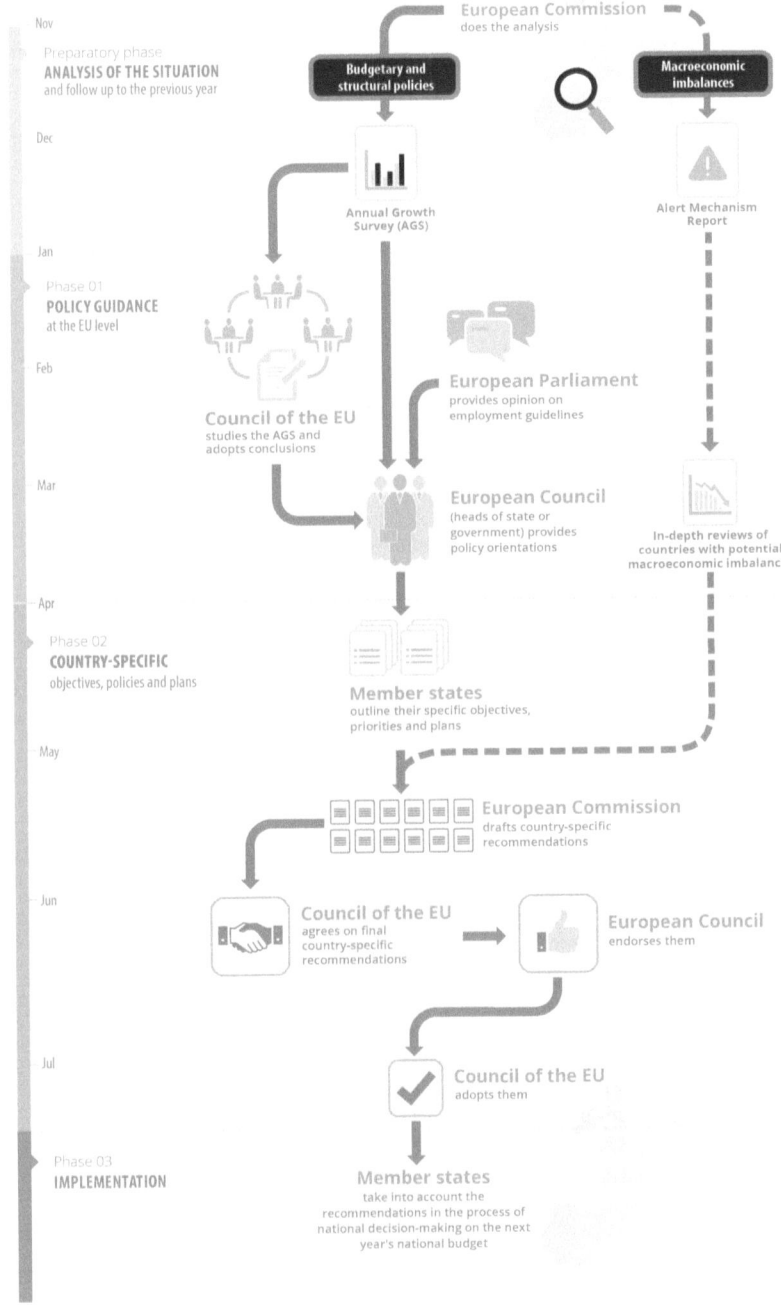

*Table 3.1* **Comparing three families of EU decision-making**

| Key Feature | Community method | Intergovernmental method | Coordinative method |
| --- | --- | --- | --- |
| Initiation | Controlled by the Commission. | Controlled by the member states via the Council and European Council. | Largely intergovernmental. While based on Commission assessment, the Council and European Council adopt both general economic guidelines and country-specific norms. |
| Legislation | Requires agreement between the member states in the form of the Council (normally qualified majority) and the European Parliament. | Agreements made by the Council, with the Commission and EP largely acting as observers. In foreign policy, unanimous agreement normally required. | Recommendations adopted via reversed qualified majority procedure. The EP has no role in adoption. |
| Form | Decisions result in legislation, judicially reviewable at the EU level, and based on enumerated competences. Legislative measures in areas outside the EU's powers may be judicially challenged. | Agreements may or may not carry the form of binding law. In foreign policy, decisions and common positions are binding for the EU and its member states; in economic governance, non-binding recommendations predominate. | Rules take the form of soft law. Recommendations may relate to areas beyond EU competence. |
| Implementation | The Commission implements EU-level measures supranationally. Some laws are implemented at the national level, though safeguarded by EU. | Member states ensure that common positions are observed. EU supervision takes place only in cases of significant non-compliance. | Remains a national responsibility but subject to intense, detailed, and escalating EU-level review. |
| Legal Effects | Binding EU measures carry presumed supremacy over conflicting national laws. | Judicial review primarily at the national level; EU-level judicial review only under limited exceptions. | EU-level review largely precluded. National judicial review of soft recommendations also limited. |
| Legitimation | Based on output and consensus. | Based on output and consensus. | Based on output. |

- **Agenda setting is mainly intergovernmental.** While based on Commission assessment, the Council and European Council adopt both general economic guidelines and country-specific norms.
- Recommendations are adopted via **a novel reversed qualified majority procedure** (i.e. are adopted unless overturned by a qualified majority of states). The EP has no role in adoption.
- **Rules take the form of soft law.** As soft norms, recommendations may often relate to areas beyond EU competence.
- Implementation **remains a national responsibility but is subject to intense, detailed, and escalating EU-level review.** Nationally, states must adopt a 'corrective mechanism' to ensure adherence to balanced budget rules. Supranationally, the Commission is authorised to monitor performance through recommendations both before and after a national budget's adoption.
- **EU-level review is largely precluded.** National judicial review of soft recommendations is also limited (see below).
- **Legitimation is output-based.** Lacking parliamentary legitimation, legitimacy is predicated on the ability of coordination to deliver economic stability. Conflicting goals, for example, social cohesion or public health, are largely evaluated through a fiscal lens.

While Table 3.1 summarises the key features of all three 'families' of EU decision-making, it may be useful here to highlight four characteristics of the coordinative method's design that make it so different.

## What makes this method coordinative?

EU economic decision-making is coordinative in that it is formed as a policy cycle based on a constant 'back and forth' between the EU and national levels. This contrasts with the more hierarchical design of both the Community and intergovernmental methods as sets of uniform rules agreed upon at the EU-level and which member states must then enforce. To highlight one example, under the Two Pack legislation, designed to prevent governments from building up deficits, member states and EU institutions engage in a never-ending cycle of budgetary monitoring (see Figure 3.1). Not only are member states obliged to submit draft budgets to EU institutions prior to their national adoption, but the Commission may request a revised budget. An inability to adopt a balanced budget leads to an escalating series of further measures, from Commission monitoring and recommendations to the possibility of financial sanctions. Unlike the Community method or intergovernmental method, decision-making never crystallises into a 'once and for all' agreement but is ongoing and revisable with the possibility of norms being adapted to changed factual circumstances.

## How is the coordinative method enforced?

While the coordinative method operates under soft law, one may question whether it is less coercive than the two other decision-making families. It may simply be that another form of coercion is in operation. Under the Community method, for example, the main form of coercion was legal. Under coordination, the form of coercion in operation is largely financial and based on repeated and prescriptive micro-interventions by EU institutions. Under both the MIP and EDP, financial sanctions in the form of an interest-bearing deposit of 0.2 per cent of GDP are possible relatively early in the decision-making process, even before an excessive deficit has been declared. While coordination thus can be seen as soft law, it is on paper much less soft than the old OMC. Major questions surrounding the future of this framework are whether these sanctions will in practice be applied, and if so, how often.

## Does the coordinative method apply equally to all EU states?

The level of coercion and monitoring to which a state is subject is not uniform across member states. Under the old Community and intergovernmental methods, states were subject to relatively uniform obligations. Under the coordinative method, the level of EU intervention depends on a state's fiscal condition. For states with balanced budgets, such as Finland or Germany, the level of central oversight is limited. For states with budget deficits, however, the coordinative method involves budgetary partnerships with EU institutions, with the EU carrying significant power to steer and alter national budgets. For states receiving financial assistance, the level of EU intervention is even greater. To paraphrase, while previous EU decision-making saw member states as sovereign equals, under the coordinative method, the level of sovereignty a state enjoys increasingly depends on its solvency (Enderlein et al. 2012: 7).

## What is the relation between EU and national governance under the coordinative method?

Finally, the coordinative method involves a significant reconfiguration of the balance of power between the EU and its member states. Not only is EU intervention more regular, but it is also deeper, extending beyond traditional areas of EU competence and including detailed, rather than general, policy prescriptions (Bekker 2013). This is borne out by an analysis of the most recent rounds of country-specific recommendations adopted in the context of the European Semester. Recommendations are increasingly made in areas going far beyond official EU competences (e.g. in pensions, tax, health, and other areas of policy) and often mention specific government programmes to be cut or altered. Many of these recommendations are similar across states, even among quite different regulatory and political models. In this sense, coordination is used in a more prescriptive and less flexible manner than before, aimed at ensuring budgetary consolidation across the euro area.

In this sense, the coordinative method seems to combine the intergovernmental decision-making structure of intergovernmentalism with the centralised and harmonising implementation structure of the Community method. The most fundamental and over-arching decisions (e.g. over the issuance of debt or the guidelines steering EU macroeconomic policy) remain with the member states, yet central institutions have gained ever greater powers in how these decisions are domestically implemented.

While national governments have demanded 'more Europe' and more supervision of the process of fiscal consolidation, they have still insisted on controlling intergovernmentally the most important levers of policy change (Fabbrini 2013, forthcoming). This uneasy marriage of supranational steering and intergovernmental control has led to a transformed EU decision-making structure.

## Evaluating Coordination: What Is It Good for, and What Is It Bad for?

How do we evaluate the coordinative method? In so far as this is a method in its infancy, it may be too early to judge its effectiveness at meeting functional demands. One can point to some preliminary dilemmas, however, along each of the four factors of change with which we began:

1. **Functionality:** Just as each crisis in the history of EU integration has led to new institutions to meet functional demands, so the euro crisis has created new European institutions and bodies. An aspect of the coordinative method is thus the delegation of implementation and supervisory powers both to the Commission, as described above, and to other technocratic bodies. While economic governance involves the determination of salient and controversial political choices, many of these choices are to be taken by politically independent bodies, empowered as a result of their technical expertise. The clearest institutional transfer of power has been to the European Central Bank (ECB). On top of its traditional function of maintaining price stability, the ECB has

been empowered during the crisis with a number of new mandates, from managing financial assistance for struggling economies to supervising the balance sheets and lending practices of large eurozone banks. A number of other new financial institutions, including the European Systemic Risk Board (ESRB) and three new EU-level agencies for the supervision of financial activities, have been added to assist the ECB in regulatory functions (Quaglia 2013). As will be explored below, the credibility of these bodies has often been staked on their independence from political steering and manipulation, hence creating considerable difficulties in rendering their decisions politically accountable.

2. **Diversity:** The addition of new EU functions has only been possible by rendering new rules and institutions inapplicable to certain states. While the earlier intergovernmental and Community methods tried to accommodate national diversity within common institutional structures, under the coordinative method, the notion that states should be subject to equal obligations has been gradually abandoned. Institutional fragmentation is the new norm (Schimmelfennig and Winzen 2014). This can be observed in the field of budgetary monitoring: Poorer and debt-laden states face greater supervision. It is also apparent in greater divisions between eurozone and non-eurozone states. Within the eurozone, states may seek to move towards greater coordination not only in fiscal policy but also in other fields likely to have an impact on the common currency (e.g. taxation, banking, consumer protection, and other areas). Such measures, however, may often prove unacceptable to non-eurozone states. As a result, we increasingly see policies such as the new financial transaction tax, institutions such as the Eurogroup and ESM, or entire treaties such as the Fiscal Compact and ESM treaties, which are applicable to some EU states but not others. This phenomenon (or other possible shifts towards a 'two-speed' Europe) is likely to cause significant coordination problems in reconciling policies applicable to the eurozone with those, such as the internal market, applicable to the EU-28 as a whole. This is a dilemma that is also likely to resonate at an institutional level, for example, when EU institutions designed to serve the whole Union are enlisted to achieve tasks tailored specifically for eurozone states.

**Fiscal Compact**

As part of the intergovernmental Treaty on Stability, Coordination and Governance (TSCG), the Fiscal Compact was signed by 25 EU member states (all except the Czech Republic, the United Kingdom, and Croatia) in March 2012 and entered into force on 1 January 2013. The treaty enhances the Stability and Growth Pact (SGP) by aiming for balanced national budgets. Member states have to enact legislation introducing a debt brake of 0.5% of GDP accompanied by automatic correction mechanisms if this limit is exceeded. Implementation is monitored by the European Commission.

3. **Effectiveness:** The development of new EU functions via the coordinative method can also be seen as a response to the perceived ineffectiveness of economic coordination prior to the crisis (cf. Chapter 2). This refers particularly to both the relatively weak levers available to EU institutions to deter non-compliance with fiscal standards as well as the limited capacity for preventive intervention before significant economic imbalances could take hold. Although, as already mentioned, it is too early to comprehensively analyse the effectiveness of the new framework, some lessons are presented by previous efforts at EU policy coordination. In the case of the aforementioned OMC, policy coordination efforts had some success in encouraging mutual learning and the sharing of best practices between member states. Coordination was less successful, however, in creating policy convergence and harmonisation around shared EU norms (Kok et al. 2004). In simple terms, while the coordinative method seems to carry enhanced incentives and sanctions to encourage compliance with EU standards, its very innovation leaves significant question marks regarding its effectiveness.
4. **Legitimacy:** Even if the coordinative method is effective, to what extent is it legitimate? While the issue of legitimacy is explored in more depth in Chapter 4, the intergovernmental and Community methods used a combination of national accountability in the former case and accountability to EU political institutions, particularly the European Parliament, in the latter case to justify democratically enhanced steering and control at the EU level. This input legitimacy was combined with the output legitimacy of delivering public goods that national governments could not provide on their own (Scharpf 2003). While the coordinative method continues to rely on output legitimacy, particularly in delivering a sustainable and balanced European economy, how does it achieve input legitimacy or even the most basic modicum of legal and political accountability? The importance and seriousness of this last question deserves further consideration.

## The Accountability Gaps of the Coordinative Method

Why is securing appropriate structures of legal and political accountability in the EU emerging from the euro crisis so important? Largely, this is owing to three factors. Firstly, the coordinative method involves EU intervention in areas far beyond the EU's treaty-based powers. The reach of recommendations under the European Semester into budgetary, social, and tax policy goes far beyond the express limitations on EU intervention in these fields as listed in the EU treaties. Secondly, such interventions involve the accrual of power over highly salient social and political areas of policy. While the EU project was designed to respect national democratic processes (cf. Art. 4(2) TEU) within which citizens remain deeply embedded, the heightened ability of the Union's executive institutions to alter or veto national budgets entails a European decision-making process able to influence, or even determine, the most basic political choices exercised in national democracies (Crum 2013). Finally, this increase in central intervention comes at a time when popular confidence and trust in the EU project and its institutions are at all-time lows (cf. Chapter 5 on governance indicators). The steep rise in support for anti-EU and extremist parties in the 2014 parliamentary elections is indicative of a paradox: An increase in EU steering is taking place precisely at the moment when the founding ideals of EU integration are being increasingly contested across the Union. These factors make securing legal and political accountability under new forms of EU decision-making particularly crucial.

How was accountability secured under the two previous decision-making 'families'? In fact, both methods contained their own mechanisms for both legal and political accountability. For the Community method, this accountability was secured primarily at the European level. Politically, for example, the activities of EU institutions, particularly the Commission, were to be monitored by the European Parliament, which was also responsible for co-deciding most EU legislation. Legally, meanwhile, the actions of EU institutions in enforcing EU norms had to be based on precise legal rules and enumerated EU competences and aimed at meeting overarching principles such as subsidiarity, proportionality, and non-discrimination, all of which could be enforced via the European courts.

For the intergovernmental method, while the involvement of the European Parliament and jurisdiction of the European Courts was often precluded, there were significant mechanisms of accountability at the national level. Politically, national governments were accountable to their national parliaments for decisions agreed upon at the EU level in areas such as common defence and security policy; in turn, many national parliaments would censure their governments where they deviated from prior-agreed mandates. Meanwhile, at the legal level, even if EU decisions in areas like defence could not be reviewed by the Court of Justice, they could be reviewed by national courts, where those decisions carried real legal effects. Under both methods, therefore, the exercise of European public power was subject to mechanisms of legal and political scrutiny at different levels.

The principal difficulty of the coordinative method may be its capacity to evade such accountability. In simple terms, while the coordinative method has allowed the EU to create new forms of authority, this authority has not necessarily been accompanied by a robust accountability structure.

## Political and parliamentary accountability

Let us start at the political level. While, as discussed above, EU economic policy has become significantly more prescriptive, this has not been matched by an extension of the powers of the European Parliament. New treaties establishing obligations for the member states such as the Fiscal Compact and ESM Treaties do not mention the Parliament; at the same time, fiscal recommendations to the member states are made by the Commission and the Council (namely, Ecofin, composed of national finance ministers) alone. While such fiscal recommendations can involve deep changes to EU and national fiscal and social policy, the body representing EU citizens directly is relegated under the coordinative method to a largely consultative role, carrying an economic dialogue with other EU institutions but no real decision-making power (Fasone 2014).

This sidelining of the European Parliament has often been matched during the crisis by a declining role in budgetary policy for national parliaments. Particularly important in this regard are the effects that new economic governance procedures are likely to have on one of the most important historical functions of parliaments: their power to control their executives through the adoption of national budgets. While on the one hand, the coordinative method provides EU institutions with significant powers with which to demand alterations to national budgets, on the other hand, it also limits the time available to parliaments to scrutinise budgetary decisions. According to one of the key regulations framing the European Semester, for example, the Commission is asked to provide its opinion on draft national budgets by 30 November, with 31 December given as the deadline for final national adoption. In this sense, parliaments are given only one month to discuss, scrutinise, and contest supranational constraints on national budgets.

Unsurprisingly, there is some evidence that these procedural constraints have led to limited national parliamentary scrutiny of EU economic governance since the European Semester was established. According to a study by Hefftler and Wessels (2013), in 2013, the national government's response to the Commission's Annual Growth Survey on national budgets was debated in the parliamentary plenary in only seven member states and at the Committee level in only two thirds of states. Reflecting the move towards different obligations for different states, one can also observe severe variations between states in the level of parliamentary scrutiny, with parliamentary debate much more likely in states with a more positive fiscal outlook. From 2011 to 2012, for example, Estonia, Finland, Denmark, Germany, Sweden, and Austria ranked highest in the overall number of ex ante committee meetings debating European Council and Euro summits. Cyprus, Greece, and Ireland were counted among those states holding no such meetings. National parliamentary scrutiny under the coordinative method seems least advanced in precisely those states that may need it most.

Finally, at a political level, political accountability is made more difficult by the aforementioned tendency to delegate powers to technocratic institutions during the crisis. As highlighted, the institutional actor gaining the most power during the crisis has been the ECB. While the ECB has already won increasing powers of micro- and macro-prudential supervision during the last three years, the political consequences of its work may significantly increase in the future. The possible need to utilise, for example, the outright monetary transactions (OMT) programme could involve significant purchases of public and governments assets (Claeys, Hallerberg, and Tschekassin 2014: 10). Such purchases are likely to benefit some states, as well as particular creditor groups within states, more than others or may even lead to conflict with other ECB functions. The gradual accrual of power within the ECB also seems to demand some political control and accountability for its actions.

> *Political accountability has been made more difficult by the tendency to delegate powers to technocratic institutions during the crisis.*

In spite of this, the ECB is one of the world's most independent central banks. As illustrated by other academic work (Claeys, Hallerberg, and Tschekassin 2014), the levels of accountability of the ECB compare unfavourably to other major central banks such as the Bank of England or the United States Federal Reserve. While the ECB's president is obliged to engage in a monetary dialogue with the European Parliament, that Parliament, unlike the US Congress, carries few mechanisms for disciplining the Bank or its members when the ECB is seen to incorrectly fulfil its treaty mandate. To focus on three prominent examples, the publication of the minutes of the ECB's governing board meetings, the ability to appoint governing board members, and the capacity to amend the Bank's statute–all powers available to the US Congress–are unavailable to the European Parliament. To this extent, while the shift of power to technocratic agencies like the ECB has been conducted for important reasons (e.g. to increase the credibility of EU economic policy), it is creating a decision-making space of unaccountable and discretionary decision-making at the EU level.

## Judicial review

If political accountability after the crisis is lacking, then what about accountability at a legal level? One of the distinctive elements of the euro crisis has been the important role of courts in reviewing crisis-related measures. One court in particular, the German Constitutional Court, has been at the forefront of this debate, its every decision carefully dissected by national and international media. This would give the impression that the EU's new economic governance is subject to close judicial scrutiny. In fact, judicial review of crisis measures is problematic at both the EU and national levels.

At the EU level, this relates to the nature of decisions under the coordinative method. As mentioned above, decisions in EU economic governance rarely take the form of clear and binding rules. Instead, governments are asked to meet certain broad guidelines and targets: For example, they are asked to avoid 'serious macro-economic imbalances' or to ensure that their budget deficits are cohering towards a 'medium-term budgetary objective' (MTO). In this way, the executive actors monitoring their behaviour–more precisely, the Commission–carry considerable discretion as to when a member state has or has not complied with a particular rule and which sanction or action to apply for non-compliance.

The nature of the coordinative method as a set of vague decisions rather than binding rules renders judicial review exceedingly difficult (Chalmers 2012). For instance, an element of the national budget that the Commission must examine is whether states carry an excessive structural deficit (i.e. a deficit that reflects underlying fiscal imbalances rather than merely fluctuations in the economic cycle). The question of how to measure the structural deficit relies on heavily contested definitions, even among economists, of which headings of expenditure should or should not be counted within this category. Such complex calculations are hardly amenable to objective judicial review. By creating such indeterminate rules, judges are likely to have little choice but to defer to the decisions of policy-makers.

This degree of indeterminacy leaves significant scope for arbitrary and/or politicised decision-making. As Chalmers and Chaves (2014) have documented, the opacity of Commission decisions under the coordinative method can be observed by the operation of the excessive deficit procedure in 2013. To contrast two states, in 2013 Belgium was asked to rectify its public deficit immediately, while France was given an extended deadline to meet its budgetary targets in spite of the fact that its deficit was 1.8 per cent above Belgium's. While there may be legitimate explanations for this particular discrepancy, this example highlights the potential for abuses of discretionary power under the coordinative method, such as the possibility that rules will apply disproportionately to smaller and politically weaker member states. Such abuses are only likely to be avoided when Courts exercise vigilance in monitoring executive activities.

The response of the European courts to the crisis so far indicates their reticence to do just this. As Hinarejos (2013, forthcoming) has pointed out, in its Pringle decision on the compatibility of the Fiscal Compact and ESM agreements with general EU treaties, the Court of Justice was reluctant to fundamentally question new institutional arrangements designed to re-enforce the stability of the euro area. While, for example, the construction of the ESM seemed to conflict with the EU treaties' prohibition of bail-outs between EU states, the Court read that clause as allowing financial assistance so long as based on strict conditionality, requiring debtor states to meet stringent terms set by their creditors. Ironically for a European court intent in the past on guaranteeing the integrity of EU fundamental rights, the Court also argued that the EU's Charter of Fundamental Rights did not apply to the decisions of the ESM's governing board (Court of Justice of the European Union 2012).

To decide otherwise, at a time where the eurozone faced severe pressure, would of course have threatened the euro's very survival. The Court's deferential approach could be defended from a constitutional perspective: Traditionally, constitutional courts have often treated fiscal and budgetary policy as an area of high political salience in which judicial actors should leave significant scope for executive and parliamentary discretion. Nonetheless, the Court's seal of approval of these measures calls into question its ability to safeguard constitutional standards and rights at times of high emergency (cf. also Chapter 4). The Court's failure to consider whether lending conditions under the ESM might threaten social rights protected under the EU Charter–a question it has repeatedly refused to answer, in spite of several references from national courts–may be an indication of its limited ability to secure EU-level judicial review.

To what extent could these difficulties in transnational legal accountability be compensated at the national level? Certainly, national courts throughout the Union have been active in questioning the compatibility of new economic governance arrangements with national constitutional frameworks (Fabbrini 2014). The capacity of national courts to exert influence on their governments, however, is certainly not equal. To make this point, one can contrast the stories of two constitutional courts, those of Germany and Portugal.

The Federal Constitutional Court of Germany has been a particularly influential institution in guiding the EU's response to the crisis in the eurozone. When considering, for example, whether to agree to the creation of the ESM, German Chancellor Merkel first insisted on a limited amendment to the EU treaties: a move widely interpreted as an attempt to placate her nation's highest court. The Court has since then decided a number of cases dealing with crisis measures, culminating in its recent decision to, for the first time ever, refer a question to the European courts on the compatibility of the ECB's latest OMT lending programme with EU treaties.

The common thread running through the German Constitutional Court's decisions has been its simultaneous insistence on, firstly, the overall compatibility of new lending arrangements with German constitutional law and secondly, on the need to introduce safeguards to protect the decision-making autonomy of the German Bundestag. In examining the ESM, for example, the Court argued that its legality was contingent upon binding guarantees whereby the German Bundestag would be fully informed and carry an effective veto over lending decisions of its governing board. In so far that it has acted to strengthen channels of accountability between executives at the EU level and those in domestic parliaments, such an approach is commendable from an accountability perspective (avoiding the obvious problem, hinted at above, of a judicial takeover of sensitive political decisions).

The problem with this approach appears when we contrast the power of the Federal Constitutional Court of Germany with its counterparts in other states (Everson and Joerges 2013). The Constitutional Court of Portugal, for example, has also often found its government's actions in relation to eurozone rescue measures wanting. In 2012, the Court found a number of measures, including cutting public wages and social entitlements, contrary to social rights protected under the Constitution of Portugal. Realising that these measures were a direct consequence of Portugal's obligations towards its external debtors, the effects of the judgment were delayed for one year. As a result, the same measures were simply re-instated by the government in the 2013 budget, with this budget once again ruled unconstitutional.

In effect, the options available to the Portuguese government are extremely limited, as is the capacity of the Portuguese Constitutional Court to alter the government's approach. Any alteration to the national budget in an effort to alleviate conflicts with social rights would be precisely in violation of the conditionality agreements made by Portugal when entering into its financial assistance programme. Here, we have a paradox: The very 'conditions' which, for Portugal, infringe the national constitution, are conditions that, for Germany and the European courts, are necessary for intra-lending to be legal.

This comparison shows the limits of national judicial review as a means of overcoming the legal accountability gaps of the coordinative method. In an environment where the levels of autonomy of European states are highly unequal, so is the likely degree of constitutional review and judicial protection. National judicial review seems no substitute for EU judicial actors, who are willing and able to call to account those changes in EU policy-making likely to impinge upon constitutional safeguards.

> *While the coordinative method has created a new form of transnational power, that power is being exercised without real mechanisms of accountability.*

In this sense, while the coordinative method has created a new form of transnational power used to steer eurozone governments towards a (hopefully) more sustainable fiscal future, that power is being exercised without real mechanisms of accountability, whether they be political or legal, national or transnational. Filling this gap may be one of the foremost challenges for EU policy-makers in the decade to come.

# Bridging the Accountability Gap

How do we fill this accountability gap? As this chapter has argued, meeting the accountability deficit requires addressing its legal and political, as well as national and supranational, dimensions. In this sense, while some previous accounts of the crisis have tried to focus on one particular institutional remedy such as the re-empowerment of national parliaments or EU-level judicial review, the argument of this chapter is that an accountable EU governance structure requires scrutiny and reform along all four dimensions. While the recommendations below are only suggestions, some of which may be more politically feasible than others, they are intended to prompt a debate about how a more holistic approach to rendering the EU's new economic governance more accountable could be developed. In short, while much of the exploratory nature of new forms of economic governance have related to a search for new functional remedies, exploratory governance may also be required to identify new mechanisms of transnational accountability.

## Political accountability: supranational

This debate should begin at a political level. When considering supranational political accountability, one of the key features of the coordinative method is its sidelining of the European Parliament in favour of various executive bodies from the ECB to the European Council. While there are clear functional rationales for this shift in power, an over-reliance on executive expertise and control carries the obvious danger of further removing EU politics from the will and preferences of EU citizens. Contrary to previous increases in EU competence, such as the Lisbon Treaty, which heralded the mainstreaming of the co-decision procedure across most fields of EU policy-making, the increase in EU steering power during the crisis has not been accompanied by heightened links to EU parliamentary decision-making.

A key recommendation of this chapter is to consider and develop steps towards 'communitarising' economic governance. It is unclear why the European Parliament, seen as fit to determine and deliberate other fields of EU policy, is so insulated from new fields of EU economic competence and high political salience. Ironically, while the recent EP elections were dominated by the issue of austerity in Europe and its boundaries, the EP carries relatively few powers to change the direction of EU economic policy.

One could imagine several possible steps to alter this trajectory. One is to increase the powers of the EP to co-determine decisions in the context of EU fiscal policy. While the Lisbon Treaty suggests that country-specific recommendations are to be adopted by the Council alone, nothing in the treaty prohibits the Council and Commission from establishing an inter-institutional agreement whereby the content of those recommendations would be fully deliberated and voted upon ex ante in either the relevant committees or the plenary of the EP. Such a role is even more justified for the adoption of budgetary partnerships between the Commission and individual member states, which have involved limited appropriations from the EU budget. Greater EP involvement in national budgetary supervision would, in simple terms, add a different set of voices to the interests currently in the driving seat of fiscal surveillance: the Commission and the Eurogroup.

Even in circumstances where the EP does not decide, it could at least adopt greater supervisory and monitoring powers over executive institutions making crucial economic decisions. A crucial actor in this regard is the ECB and its associated agencies. As Michele Everson has highlighted, banking union is increasingly likely to involve the technocratic imposition of choices that have significant distributive consequences (Everson forthcoming). Recommendations in this regard could be to increase the level of EP control over the membership of the ECB and its supervisory board, as well as to more regularly interrogate the president of the Bank and the heads of regulatory agencies over their role in macro-economic supervision (cf. Claeys, Hallerberg, and Tschekassin 2014). This enhanced scrutiny power could extend to asking the presidents of the European Council and the Eurogroup to appear before the EP both before and after European Council and Euro summits (Piedrafita and Blockmans 2014: 20). Greater accountability to the EP for the agenda of European Council meeting outcomes could contribute to recasting the EU's shift towards enhanced executive power.

## Political accountability: national

The enhancement of political accountability should also take place at the national level. As this chapter has also highlighted, one of the main impacts of the crisis has been the loss of traditional parliamentary monopoly power over the agreement of national budgets. While restoring this monopoly seems politically and economically infeasible, national parliaments certainly have a right to not only have a say in the implementation of EU fiscal policy, but also to play a role in its formation. This is particularly so for the parliaments of smaller and poorer member states who, as highlighted above, have often been disempowered via the crisis.

An important recommendation in this regard is to follow through on the promise contained in Article 13 of the Fiscal Compact of an Inter-Parliamentary Conference on Economic and Financial Governance. A first conference, bringing together national parliamentarians with relevant EP committees, took place in Lithuania in October 2013. As highlighted by others (cf. Cooper 2014), that conference was beset by disagreements between the EP and national parliamentarians, with the conference ultimately unable to adopt binding rules of procedure. This failure speaks in part to the EP's resistance to the creation of bodies of inter-parliamentary cooperation that could be seen as competing with the EP for the right to represent the interests of citizens at the EU level.

Taking the disempowerment of national parliaments via the crisis seriously would involve dropping such opposition to inter-parliamentary cooperation. Parliaments at both national and EU levels have a strong common interest in resisting the drift of budgetary control from a parliamentary to a largely executive prerogative and in ensuring that the operation and timetabling of the European Semester allows full parliamentary scrutiny of budgetary proposals. A strong Article 13 conference, held on dates coordinated with major decision points in the European Semester, such as the Commission's release of its Annual Growth Survey, and able to formulate recommendations and opinions could go some way towards re-balancing how power under EU economic governance is exercised.

## Legal accountability: supranational

While enhancing political accountability is a crucial task, political advances also need to be underpinned by legal commitments. As discussed above, a crucial element of the coordinative method has been the difficulty in securing judicial review of its activities at either the supranational or national level. At the supranational level, this begins with ensuring that EU economic governance remains subject to the legal and due process guarantees established under the EU treaties. The treatment, highlighted by Alicia Hinarejos (forthcoming) and others, of instruments such as the ESM as being 'outside the scope of EU law' may make it more difficult to subject major new fields of EU action to judicial scrutiny. This exclusion of jurisdiction by the EU courts is difficult to justify, given the heavy involvement of EU institutions, particularly the European Commission, in ESM decisions such as the conditionality attached to financial bail-outs to struggling member states.

A first recommendation would therefore be for the EU courts to more carefully consider the links between EU economic governance and other elements of EU law. It is difficult to justify why decisions under EU economic governance made by the EU institutions should not be fully subject to the EU Charter of Fundamental Rights, including the social and due process rights contained therein. In this regard, national courts asking the Court of Justice for guidance on the compatibility of conditionality decisions with the broader framework of EU law deserve better than the EU courts' refusal to answer preliminary references to date. The European courts must not avoid but face head on their responsibility to ensure that the EU's policy-making structure, in all of its aspects, properly conforms to the wider EU treaties.

A second recommendation in this regard relates to a more specific problem. As discussed above, the coordinative method has often involved significant differentiation between states, with the eurozone increasingly adopting agreements, such as the Fiscal Compact, that were not agreed to by other member states. This creates the possibility of conflict between rules and policies agreed by the eurozone and those made by the larger EU. A second crucial recommendation would be to make greater use of EU law as a forum to mediate conflicts between the EU's euro 'core' and its larger membership.

This would involve, for example, designing safeguards–some of which have already been agreed–for non-participating states in new economic governance arrangements for the eurozone. This could involve an agreement (Piedrafita and Blockmans 2014) to place limits on the ability of member states to sign international treaties outside the ordinary EU framework. A model for the types of guarantees that this agreement could include can already be found within the existing treaties. Articles 326 to 334 of the TFEU, for example, try to ensure that when a limited number of governments agree upon measures of secondary legislation, they have to meet certain safeguards such as ensuring that the common market is not affected, that a minimum number of states participate, and that participating states first made reasonable efforts to agree under the normal Community method. Extending these guarantees to international treaties initiated outside the EU framework would be a useful first step in preventing constitutional tensions in a more differentiated integration project.

## Legal accountability: national

Finally, legal accountability under the coordinative method must also be secured at the national level. This chapter has discussed the asymmetries between national courts, some of which have exercised rigorous judicial review designed to strengthen their domestic institutions, alongside other judicial systems that have been significantly disempowered. In the former case, actions by powerful national courts can have destabilising influences when those actions influence significantly and unilaterally the direction of EU law and policy. There may be two elements to addressing this imbalance.

The first element relates to the relationship between national and EU courts. National constitutional courts in large member states should be encouraged to refer issues that concern not just national but also wider EU constitutional law to the European courts for consideration by a judicial body designed to apply European law for the benefit of the whole of the European continent. While many have criticised the robust phrasing of the Federal Constitutional Court of Germany's recent reference to the Court of Justice on the legality of the ECB's OMT programme, the Constitutional Court should be applauded for making its first-ever reference to the Court of

Justice. An ongoing dialogue between EU and national legal orders is a vital ingredient for building a common constitutional order for Europe through which tensions between national and EU standards can be worked through and resolved.

Secondly, however, judicial dialogue must extend not just upwards to the EU level, but also horizontally between national courts. A frequent criticism of German jurisprudence, for example, has been its unwillingness to consider the impact of its decisions (Everson and Joerges 2013) on other jurisdictions. A logical corollary of the 'duty of sincere cooperation' contained in Art. 4 of the TEU is surely an obligation on national courts to take into account the constitutional principles and rights of other member states. Full participation of national high court judges in institutions designed to promote transnational judicial dialogue, such as Eurojust and the Network of President of the Supreme Judicial Courts of the EU (NPSJC), would certainly ease this process (de Visser and Claes 2013), as would further steps designed to facilitate the easy access to national judgments (e.g. the electronic filing and translation of important national judgments).

These steps, even if taken in concert, would be no immediate panacea for the complex trade-offs between legitimacy and efficiency, or between the rule of law and EU governance (to be explored in the following chapter), that the euro crisis has created. In keeping with the framework of exploratory governance discussed in Chapter 1, improvements in EU governance are likely to be contingent and incremental, revealing new problems of legal and political accountability in their place. What is offered here are merely suggestions as to how a more politically responsive and legally sound EU governance structure could be found, given the radically heightened ambitions of EU policy outlined in this Report. As will be explored in Chapter 4, the search for new avenues of legal and political accountability are vital, given the deep problems of democratic and constitutional legitimacy created by the crisis and the EU's response to it.

# IV. The Legitimacy *Problématique* of Economic Governance in the EU

CHRISTIAN JOERGES

A spectre is haunting Europeanists. The spectre is German ordo-liberalism, a school of thought that synthesises legal principles and economic science in a prescriptive modelling of market economies. Ordo-liberalism–it is alleged–is inspiring the crisis politics that the European Union (EU)'s most powerful member state has been orchestrating through the imposition of budgetary discipline and austerity politics. The spectre's precursor is another story with German origins, albeit a more comforting one. This story is about the 'social market economy', a successful coordination of an efficient competitive market economy and social justice in the formative phase of the Federal Republic. The concept, so the story goes, not only shaped the wording of the draft Constitutional Treaty of the European Convention and the Treaty of Lisbon (Art. 3(3) TEU) but nearly became the ideational paradigm of a European social model until it was betrayed by the EU's turn to austerity politics.

> The successful governance of the economy and the provision of social justice are the two core commitments of Europe's post-war democracies.

The attention that both narratives attract may be an understandable consequence of the type of memory politics that the present crisis has provoked in Greece and elsewhere (cf. Kundnani 2014) and that had been important in the move towards a common currency, in particular for France and Germany (cf. Dyson 2014: 612 ff.). But they are flawed. Why attempt to correct both the nightmare and the fairy tale in a chapter on the legitimacy *problématique* of the European integration project? The reasons are threefold:

- The first is normative. The successful governance of the economy and the provision of social justice are the two core commitments of Europe's post-war democracies. Implicit in the two narratives, however, is the message that Europe has not been able to preserve the post-war legacy of democratic constitutionalism. Thus, the European project would now need to find an alternative model on which to base its legitimacy.

- The second reason is analytical and critical. The flaws of the two narratives mirror the institutional deficits of the European construct, an analysis that implies a twofold critique of European constitutionalism: firstly, that the political dimension of the economy has been treated too complacently and secondly, that the tensions between the integration of the formerly national European economies and the integration of European societies have been downplayed.
- The third is programmatic. Both of these points need to be understood within a broader theoretical framework, in this case provided by Habermas (1996) in his *Discourse Theory of Law and Democracy*. A core message of that theory concerns the relationship between the *Rechtsstaat* (rule of law) and democracy. In order to 'deserve recognition' (Habermas 2003: 188), public rule must be embedded in a legal and institutional framework that ensures the formation of democratic will and the accountability of those who govern. Since Habermas first entered into the discussion of European integration (Habermas 1991: 500-7)), his conceptual framework has remained unchanged in the basic commitment to democratic will formation and the potential of democratic rule to respond to concerns of social justice. His vision of 'transnational democracy' (Habermas 2014) and the agenda of conflicts-law constitutionalism introduced in this chapter are distinct. Nevertheless, the conflicts-law idea preserves three Habermasian cornerstones: the primacy of political democracy over the economy, the commitment to social justice, and the co-originality of the rule of law and democracy.

The three sections of this chapter will deal with these elements separately. The first section focuses on European economic governance and reconstructs the impact of ordo-liberal ideas, their normative flaws, and their defeat in and post-Maastricht. The following section highlights the tensions between European economic governance and the welfare state legacy and explains that the EU did not establish a 'social market economy'. The concluding section presents the concept of conflicts-law constitutionalism as an alternative reconstruction of legitimate European rule and explores prospects for a renewal of Europe's legitimacy.

# European Economic Governance and Its Transformations: From Rome to Maastricht

The long shadow of ordoliberalism' is the title of a much-cited paper by Sebastian Dullien and Ulrike Guérot (2012) that seeks to discern the ideational basis of 'Germany's approach to the Euro crisis'. This paper has made a wider public aware of a school of thought whose influence on German politics and the European integration process is hardly known or poorly understood in integration studies both outside and within German academic quarters. The attention that ordo-liberalism is now attracting often suffers from misunderstandings which then lead to misplaced assessments. Ordo-liberalism originated in the turmoil of the Weimar Republic, survived the Nazi period, flourished in post-war Germany, and has remained influential in German politics and institutions. The intellectual history of such a timespan is bound to be multifaceted and to undergo changes imposed or facilitated by the context in which the theory operates. In the present context, three features that have been under-evaluated or neglected by many commentators deserve particular attention:

1. One is the co-originality of law and economics in the ordo-liberal tradition, an aspect of utmost importance for the concept of *Ordnungspolitik* in general and the project of an economic constitution in particular. This intrinsic relationship is also a feature that distinguishes the tradition from other strands of economic liberalism, especially Chicago-style law and economics (Mestmäcker 2007).[1]
2. The second is the discrepancy between the first and second generations of ordo-liberal scholarship. The schism could already be observed in the 1930s and became practically relevant in the 1970s and 1980s in Germany and Europe: It differentiates between whether competition law and policy should seek to control economic power or legislation and regulatory politics that could be considered anti-competitive.
3. The third is the law-politics relationship. The very idea of a law-bound ordering of the economy requires that all actions of the state be bound to general, constitutionally guaranteed legal principles; this implies that economic policy must be based upon 'justiciable criteria' (Mestmäcker 1973; Vanberg 2014). The managerial mode of Europe's responses to the crisis and even the construction of the economic and monetary union (EMU) are irreconcilable with these requirements.

The following reconstruction of these points is not meant as a *l'art-pour-l'art* exercise in conceptual history, let alone a defence of the ordo-liberal tradition. Its objective is, instead, to reveal failures in Europe's institutional design and politics.

## The integration through law project and its ordo-liberal ally

The foundational steps of the European project are, for very good reason, understood as a civilising response to Germany's bellicose past and the bitter experiences of many Europeans. However, post-war political leaders and Europe's citizens were also committed to overcoming the legacy of economic nationalism and the social hardships of capitalism. These latter aspects were treated with somewhat benign neglect in the early years of the European Economic Community (EEC). It took several decades until Joseph H. H. Weiler defined peace, prosperity, and supranationalism as the three constitutive ideals of the integration project (Weiler 1994), with supranationalism denominating the establishment of a collective responsibility and the taming of national interest. This depiction of the foundational European constellation captures the interdependence of the 'economic', the 'social', and the challenges of diversity while putting the economy on a firm footing. Yet, the early years were characterised by a common dedication to law as the core of the European project and an admiration for the jurisprudence of the European Court of Justice (ECJ, after 2009 renamed the Court of Justice of the European Union, CJEU). In the 1960s, the ECJ managed to assign constitutional validity to the principles of 'direct effect' and 'supremacy' in order to establish itself as the ultimate authority in the interpretation of European law and grant economic rights to European market citizens.

Reliance on law was to remain the trademark of the European project for many years to come. The famous formula of law as the 'object and the agent of integration' (Dehousse and Weiler 1990: 243) was coined as late as 1990. 'Integration through law' was both a concept and a strategy that disregarded law's societal functions and its embeddedness in social norms. Since the commitment to 'more integration' was unquestioned, with 'law' providing a normative means for its promotion, the promotion of the project through ever more legal harmonisation and uniformity was widely accepted. The methodological solipsism of the formative years, the doctrinal rigidity, and its formalism all enabled transnational interactions by a European community of lawyers and in legal scholarship long before social scientists started to take Europe seriously. The price to be paid for this kind of progress would become apparent only with the various rounds of enlargement and the continually increasing socio-economic diversity and political salience of integrationist moves. Integration through law rests upon a 'one-size-fits-all' assumption, which would become an even more inadequate response to European diversity. The promotion of more unity as an end in itself would become an increasingly insufficient response to the quest for the legitimacy of European rule.

For all these reasons it is also worth noting that 'integration through law' had, without being aware of it, a theoretically sophisticated and politically influential ally: ordo-liberalism. This school of thought had become powerful in post-war Germany, not least due to its commitment to a competitive market order that law was to respect and protect. Its success was due also to its religious roots and sensitivity to the 'social question' (Manow 2001a), which paved the way for the synthesis of economic liberalism and social policy and was to become the trademark of the Federal Republic and its 'social market economy' (Glasman 1996: 52 ff.).

An essential element of the ordo-liberal creed is the belief in non-majoritarian institutions, such as a strong antitrust authority and an independent central bank. Non-majoritarian institutions were understood as the backbone of a free market, shielding it against the self-destruction of competitive market structures, the abuse of economic power, the pursuit of short-term advantages, and fiscal policies that would put the stability of economy and society at risk. Economic freedoms (understood as constitutional rights), the co-originality and interdependence of the legal framework, and the free functioning of markets would generate the 'economic constitution' and foster the commitment to an Ordnungspolitik that both respected and protected these principles (cf. Eucken 1989; Böhm 1989). Nevertheless, ordo-liberalism was not unchallenged in Germany. In a 1957 judgment, Germany's Federal Constitutional Court held that Germany's Basic Law was not committed to a particular economic model (e.g. that of ordo-liberalism), but rather entrusted the democratically legitimated legislature with the ordering of economy and society. Even more disquieting for ordo-liberals, however, was the resurfacing of elements of the German traditions of 'organised capitalism' and 'corporatism', which was witnessed under the chancellorship of Konrad Adenauer and which had never really faded away (Abelshauser 2004: 50 ff.).

> **Direct Effect**
>
> In general, under the doctrine of direct effect, EU law can take direct effect without being integrated into national law. This applies to all binding EU laws, including treaties, secondary legislation, and international agreements, as long as the obligations are precise, clear, and unconditional and do not call for additional measures, either national or European. However, different types of secondary legislation are treated differently in terms of direct effect. Whilst regulations always apply directly, directives must first be transposed into national law by member states. Court decisions can take direct effect for a member state if specifically addressed. International agreements may also fall under the doctrine if they meet the criteria noted above. In addition to this general understanding, there is also a narrower interpretation of the direct effect doctrine. In the 1963 Van Gend en Loos judgment, the European Court of Justice ruled that individuals may also sue for rights granted by EU treaties if they satisfy the aforementioned criteria and do not require further action.

Under such circumstances, the negotiations surrounding the creation of the EEC provided a new window of opportunities. However, this window had to be opened. In its preparatory stages, European integration had been anything but an uncontested project in the ordo-liberal school (Wegmann 2002). Then, the ordo-liberal Minister of the Economy and father of the German *Wirtschaftswunder* Ludwig Erhard and the pro-European Chancellor

Konrad Adenauer agreed upon the same person to represent Germany in the European treaty negotiations: Alfred Müller-Armack, a prominent member of Adenauer's party and head of the *Grundsatzabteilung* in Erhard's ministry. Small wonder that the EEC Treaty received an ordo-liberal imprint.

Ultimately, ordo-liberals interpreted the freedoms guaranteed in the Treaty of Rome, the opening up of national economies, the anti-discrimination rules, and the commitment to a system of undistorted competition as principled 'decisions' for the establishment and competitive ordering of a free market economy. In this reading, the Community acquired a legitimacy of its own. The validity of Europe's economic governance was not dependent upon a foundational political democratic act. To the contrary, the EEC was perceived as a non-majoritarian settlement par excellence; its competitive order was based upon law and shielded against political influence (Wigger 2008). Interpreting the pertinent treaty provisions as prescribing a law-based order committed to guaranteeing economic freedoms and protecting competition by supranational institutions resolved the legitimacy problématique elegantly. The legitimacy of the economic 'ordo' was independent of the state's democratic constitutional institutions. It could also be argued that it imposed limits upon the Community and that discretionary economic policies were illegitimate and unlawful (cf. Mestmäcker 1973).

Against this background, it is comprehensible that the constitutionalisation of the treaty provisions promoted by the ECJ through the doctrines of 'direct effect' and 'supremacy' and the conceptualisation of economic freedoms as basic rights were very much to the liking of the protagonists of ordo-liberalism. The EEC Treaty promised to realise what Germany's Federal Constitutional Court had refused to accept: namely, the assignment of constitutional validity to the core principles of an ordo-liberal 'economic constitution'. Again, the alliance between economic constitutionalism and the core doctrines of the ECJ was hardly noticed by the two allies or elsewhere in European law scholarship.

## Reconceptualising ordo-liberalism

In the 1980s, the integration project gained new momentum under Commission President Jacques Delors, to whom Europe owes its renaissance through the legendary internal market programme (CEC 1985). Support was phenomenal in so many European political quarters, possibly due to the programme's ambivalence: It could be interpreted as an effort to strengthen and prioritise the institutionalisation of economic rationality in the integration project (Joerges 1994). The new emphasis on the principle of mutual recognition and the strengthening of the four freedoms as a result of ECJ decisions could be interpreted as a framework that would further processes of regulatory competition thereby subjecting national legislation to economic rationality criteria (BMWi 1986). The ECJ's readiness to supervise national legislation was complemented by new developments in competition law and policy. The attention shifted from market failures to regulatory failures and from the control of the anticompetitive practices of private actors to the control of anticompetitive regulation and state aid. The plea for de-regulation and privatisation followed with compelling logic.

Although this reorientation was incompatible with the original agenda of the ordo-liberal school, traditional ordo-liberalism had already been revised in the late 1960s by its leading exponents, whose theoretical allegiance shifted from Walter Eucken to Friedrich August von Hayek. Eucken represented the belief in a strong policing of markets through competition law as informed by economic science (Wigger 2008: 65 ff.) and a dedication to 'perfect competition'. Von Hayek underlined the spontaneity of competitive processes and held its purpose-oriented supervision to be impossible and counter-productive, relying on a mere 'pretence of knowledge' (von Hayek 1989). His *Wettbewerb als Entdeckungsverfahren* [Competition as discovery procedure] (von Hayek 2002) became the manifesto of a new generation of scholars working in the ordo-liberal tradition. Regardless of the legal and policy implications of the revised theoretical framework, the second generation remained faithful to the ordo-liberal tradition in one important sense: The framework within which the integration project should develop further remained apolitical, subjected to neither political debate nor deliberation. This framework continued to institutionalise economic liberties and economic rationality, but more flexibly and comprehensively than the original ordo-liberal school. It therefore was perceived in more recent ordo-liberal quarters as a further step towards a 'European economic constitution'.

**Supremacy**
The supremacy doctrine of the precedence of European law ensures the superiority of EU law over national law. The doctrine responds to challenges presented by conflicting European and national laws as the Union moved toward the common market. Supremacy applies to all European acts. The principle of supremacy was established by the European Court of Justice in its 1964 Costa v. ENEL judgment, in which the Court ruled that Community law must be integrated into national legal systems. In cases of conflicting laws, the European provision must be applied by all national authorities; the national law thereby loses its binding force.

This perception was wishful and naïve for two reasons. First, what had started out as a collective effort to strengthen Europe's competitiveness through new deregulatory strategies soon led to the entanglement of the EU in more policy fields and the development of increasingly sophisticated regulatory machinery. The concern of European legislation and the Commission with 'social regulation' (e.g. health and safety of consumers, safety at work, and environmental protection) in particular proved to be irrefutable. The weight and dynamics of these policy fields had been thoroughly underestimated by proponents of the economic constitution. In the end, the internal market programme was not a one-dimensional neoliberal project. The second factor concerned the economic and monetary union (EMU), which looked on paper like a consummation of the ordo-liberal project of a European economic constitution. To this second reason, we now turn in more detail.

## Economic and monetary union

'One market, one money!' The plea captured by the slogan used by the Commission in 1990 in 'An Evaluation of the Potential Benefits and Costs of Forming an Economic and Monetary Union' (DG ECFIN 1990) was successful. The common currency's performance first seemed smooth, then stagnant and jolty, and finally disastrous. Initially, however, the project of the common currency was not only marketed by the Commission but was also more widely perceived as a continuation and deepening of the integration project: a move towards 'an ever closer union'. In hindsight, we have become aware of the EMU's design defects and the difficulties in coping with their painful impacts.

### *The judicial fiction of a 'stability community'*

The lead in the debate on Europe in general and the economic and monetary union in particular has moved from law to political science and now to economics. Nonetheless, the law and its institutions deserve to be taken seriously for both factual and normative reasons that can be illustrated by analysing the Maastricht Decision of the German Constitutional Court, which was handed down in 1993 and opened the way to Germany's ratification of the Treaty. The pertinent passages on EMU state that the substantive and institutional substitution of politics and policies by legal rules was nothing less than a sine qua non for Germany's participation in the union. This assertion was in response to the argument that the EU was about to acquire such wide-ranging competences that nation states could no longer act as the masters of their democratic statehood. Economic integration, the Court stated, was an autonomous and apolitical process that must take place beyond the reach of member state political influence. By virtue of a constitutional commitment to price stability and rules that guarded against inappropriate budgetary deficits, the EMU was correctly structured. Accordingly, all doubts about the democratic legitimacy of economic integration were diverted. To rephrase the argument: Yes, the Treaty is compatible with German Basic Law, but only because it was inspired by Germany's stability philosophy and only as long as that philosophy is actually respected.

The judgment reports that it had been pointed out to the Court by 'important observers', including the president of the *Bundesbank*, Helmut Schlesinger, 'that a currency union, especially between States which are oriented towards an active economic and social policy, can ultimately only be realised in common with a political union (embracing all essential economic functions) and cannot be realised independently thereof or as a mere preliminary stage on the way to it' (BVerfGE 1993).² Can we assume that the judges were so naïve as to believe in the autonomy and sustainability of a European 'stability community'? The judges were fully aware of the fragility of the 'stability community' (Böckenförde 2010): 'The decision to agree on a monetary union and put it into operation without a simultaneous or immediately subsequent political union is a political one, for which the institutions with competence on the matter must take political responsibility' (BVerfGE 1993, translation by author).

One remains perplexed. The judges must have been aware of the impossibility of politically correcting at a later stage the deal to which they had given their legal blessing. They decided accordingly when confronted with the request to prevent the EMU from entering the third stage (BVerfGE 1998; cf. Biedenkopf 2012: 78-92). The common currency had created financial interdependencies in an ever more socio-economically heterogeneous European Union. The new exclusive European competence for monetary policy was too weak to govern the European economic sphere but strong enough to deprive member states of crucially important governmental powers. Europe continued to be a 'market without a state', while the former masters of the treaties had become 'states without markets' (Joerges 1996).

> *The common currency had created financial interdependencies in an ever more socio-economically heterogeneous European Union.*

The Court failed to consider that its judgment not only concerned Germany but also affected the entire EU. Precisely this kind of external effect of national decision-making has to be avoided in a union of equals (see below on the conflicts-law approach). One may of course concede that it would have been extremely delicate to disapprove what had been decided and approved politically, yet its solemn proclamation of a 'stability community' created a legal fiction. Neither the Treaty of Maastricht nor the later Stability and Growth Pact (SGP) provided for mechanisms to enforce its conceptual basis. The whole new regime was dependent on good economic luck and constant political bargaining.

The fragility of the 'stability community' became obvious when such central players as Germany, France, and the Netherlands did not comply with the SGP in the early 2000s and the Commission's much vaunted efforts to take action dwindled to nothing (Joerges 2005: 476-8). After unification, Germany's debt was enormous, and the interest rates set by the European Central Bank (ECB) were too onerous. Germany became the 'sick man of Europe'. Chancellor Schröder turned to austerity politics and lost the next elections (cf. Manow 2001b). It has, nevertheless, become routine to assign the failure of the EMU to non-compliance with its rules and to conclude that such laxity would in the future have to be impeded by stricter economic governance. An alternative, more honest, and more intriguing interpretation would attribute non-compliance to the economic, social, and political costs of the enforcement of a regime that represented an ill-defined political compromise rather than a sustainable constitutional settlement. As Deakin observed, 'The framework of economic governance initially established at Maastricht in 1992 and subsequently embedded in the Stability and Growth Pact of 1997 was fundamentally asymmetrical. ... The problem was growing divergence at the level of the real economy' (Deakin 2014: 88, 95). The imbalances that led to the crisis could not have been avoided if there had been stricter enforcement prior to the crisis, an analysis akin to that presented in the following section in somewhat unusual terminology.

### *The Maastricht EMU as 'diagonal conflict'*

What the president of the *Bundesbank* had argued in the Maastricht litigation is now common wisdom: The separation of monetary policy from fiscal and economic policy was bound to create irresolvable tensions. This negative assessment does not tell us, however, how we should characterise what was actually established. The EMU was a 'political compromise', writes Sergio Fabbrini (forthcoming, 2013)–an inadequate one, as Enderlein adds in Chapter 2–implying that the Maastricht deal does not provide legal guidance. It was a 'contractual arrangement', comments Albert Weale (forthcoming), meaning that Maastricht could only function via commitments anchored in the involvement of domestic constituencies. Mark Dawson, in Chapter 3 of this Report, situates the EMU in an uncharted space between the two tracks of the Community method and the intergovernmental mode of decision-making. All of these observers agree that the decoupling of monetary policy from national fiscal and economic policy has created an unruly space beyond the reach of law and European policy-making. Conceptually we can characterise the compromise as a hybrid, born in a purely political compromise between the French political *planification* and the German preference for the *ordo* of the economy (cf. Enderlein, Chapter 2 of this Report). I suggest that the specifics of the Maastricht settlement can be best characterised as a 'diagonal conflict', a notion that needs further explanation.

> *Conflicts between monetary policy at the EU level and economic or fiscal policy at the national level are of a different nature: 'diagonal'.*

Under the Maastricht Treaty, monetary policy became an exclusive competence of the EU, whereas economic and fiscal policy remained the competence of national authorities. Externalities related to the exercise of economic and fiscal policy can lead to 'horizontal' conflicts among member states, but conflicts between monetary policy at the EU level and economic or fiscal policy at the national level are of a different nature: 'diagonal'. This was already evident soon after the Maastricht Treaty was signed, when member states felt that European monetary policy did not respond adequately to their specific difficulties and interests. It was not possible for the EU to invoke the supremacy doctrine against disobedient states because the interdependence between European and national competences had been left in limbo. Both the Union and its member states are certainly interested in the functioning of the economy, but the various powers needed to accomplish this objective are attributed to two distinct levels of governance. The accommodation foreseen in Article 119 TFEU is 'the adoption of an economic policy which is based on the close coordination of Member States' economic policies' as substantiated in Article 121 TFEU. Yet, this mechanism does not resolve the tensions and was not designed with such ambitions. Each member state has distinct fiscal and economic policy preferences. This was not just an unfortunate failure but also one that reflects the structural socioeconomic differences and varieties of capitalism in the EU.

The benefits of characterising the tensions inherent in the EMU as a diagonal conflict constellation are threefold. The first benefit is analytical. The notion of diagonal conflicts depicts a specific conflict constellation in the European multilevel system of governance that should be distinguished from vertical conflicts between the EU and its member states, on the one hand, and horizontal conflicts between the member states, on the other. The notion also helps us to understand why uniform rules for solving such conflicts are simply unavailable as long as European diversity persists.

The second benefit is a better understanding of the failure of the 'integration through law' project and the need for a reconfiguration of the law-politics relationship. The coordination of monetary, fiscal, and economic policy occurs in constitutional democracies through political processes with political actors who can be held accountable. A procedural legal framework within which coordination takes the diversity of Europe's economies and societies into account has not and cannot be established in conformity with standards of democratic accountability under the Maastricht rules.

The third benefit is an easier understanding of the difficulties and deficiencies of the European praxis. Responses to the eurozone crisis provide a dramatic illustration. Their description as a 'constitutional mutation' (Tuori and Tuori 2014: 119 ff.) seems somewhat euphemistic. To be sure, such a view acknowledges that the Maastricht regime was flawed and unsustainable and that the need for legal change was hence irrefutable. Does this, however, imply that the new constellation brought about by European crisis politics deserves to be called a constitutional transformation that merits recognition? EU member states are no longer equals; 'strict conditionality' of financial aid (Art. 136(3) TFEU) can deprive states 'in difficulties' of polities in which the elected representative bodies have any significant voice. All this is normatively and politically problematic. Mark Dawson's characterisation in Chapter 3 of Europe's new modes of economic governance as the 'coordinative method' is a description that underlines the need to organise a variety of actors at all levels of governance, but it does not suggest that this new constellation would deserve normative recognition.

In summary, it seems hardly possible to characterise EMU as an accomplishment of constitutional validity (Joerges 1994, 2005). An ordo-liberal imprint is clearly visible in the commitment to price stability, the establishment of an independent central bank, the prohibition of monetary financing, the prohibition of bailouts, and the objectives of the SGP (Feld 2012). However, this framework was by no means credible. It could not ensure that member states would make use of their fiscal autonomy so that the stability philosophy would actually be respected (Feld 2011; Konrad 2014). The notion of diagonal conflicts is again illuminating. The 'one-size-fits-no-one' dilemma established through the EMU cannot be subjected to the rule of law.

There is of course nothing unusual or inherently problematic with compromises in legal texts. What is specific about the Maastricht Treaty and what distinguishes the European order from that of constitutional democracies, however, is the lack of a political infrastructure and institutional framework in which democratic political contestation could continue and legitimate a completion or improvement of what had been agreed. In the complex bargaining processes and compromises generated by the EMU, it is simply not possible to identify and hold responsible actors accountable. As the Court of Justice Advocate General wrote in his opinion on the outright monetary transaction (OMT) case: 'The division that EU law makes between those policies is a requirement imposed by the structure of the Treaties and by the horizontal and vertical distribution of powers within the Union, but in economic terms it may be stated that any monetary policy measure is ultimately encompassed by the broader category of general economic policy' (CJEU 2015: para. 129).

*In the complex bargaining processes and compromises generated by the EMU, it is simply not possible to identify and hold responsible actors accountable.*

The delineation that the Treaty's text expects us to make when characterising measures as monetary rather than economic policy has to rely on 'the objectives ascribed to that policy' (para. 127). In contrast to facts, which can be ascertained when a decision is being taken, it is usually uncertain and controversial whether such objectives can be recognised at all and, if so, how. If both the EU and its member states have a say in these matters, the characterisation of disagreements as diagonal conflicts with inherent political dimensions seems adequate. Furthermore, it is difficult to see how such conflicts can be legitimately resolved by the judiciary.

In order to evaluate the legitimacy of European rule more comprehensively, we should first complement our review of the state of the EU with a discussion of the European social model, described in Article 3(3) TEU as a 'highly competitive social market economy, aiming at full employment and social progress'.

## Social Integration

In post-war Europe, the responsibility for ensuring welfare, balancing social inequalities, and creating infrastructure for economic development has become a common feature of the nation state with constitutive importance for its social legitimacy (Leibfried and Zürn 2005; Judt 2010: 127 ff.). The choice of the Treaty of Rome for an 'economic Europe', rather than a social and political community, does not militate against that assumption. The modesty of the economic objective had facilitated negotiations considerably, and was not an assault on the turn to welfare states in post-war Europe. National social models were expected to coexist peacefully as European economies gradually integrated. The 'Ohlin Report', commissioned by the International Labour Organization (1956), had endorsed the welfare-enhancing credentials of the EEC, and Ruggie's theory of 'embedded liberalism' later provided plausible arguments for the compatibility of open borders with the preservation of social accomplishments (Ruggie 1982). *Tempora mutantur*, however. Some twenty years later, Scharpf reconstructed the previous decades as a decoupling of the common but nationally-institutionalised European social legacy from the common European 'system of undistorted competition' and lamented that integration could not compensate for this decoupling (Scharpf 2002, 2010). The breaking up of the formerly interdependent economic and social orders that ordo-liberalism had envisaged in Germany seemed unavoidable at the European level, and the European legal machinery was indeed favouring the 'marketisation' of ever more social spheres (cf. Höpner 2014).

### Between national political autonomy and market integration

Countless examples from encounters of European law with regulatory concerns of member states confirm the decoupling thesis. In many instances, the European market-building agenda intrudes into spaces that the member states have exempted from market governance on the grounds of competences that they have not, or have only partly, conferred to the European level. The tensions between European monetary policy and national fiscal and economic policy discussed above provide the most spectacular illustration. Such diagonal conflict constellations, in which European law cannot claim supremacy but must tolerate national autonomy, are 'normal' in a polity in which the 'Masters of the Treaty' have conferred sovereignty only in limited fields. In such constellations, the two levels of governance need to coordinate agendas.

In many complex conflict constellations, the ECJ has found such solutions. For example, one can defend restrictive practices in 'trade agreements' as per se legitimate mechanisms of social policy and exempt them from European competition law, provided they are fair and not abusive in their composition and rates (CJEU 1999a, b). One can also reconcile the political autonomy of local government in the provision of public transport with the freedom of services (CJEU 2003). To take the most recent example, it is conceivable for national measures against climate change to survive in the European electricity market (CJEU 2014b). In its responses, the Court had to depart from the 'one-size-fits-all' philosophy and resort instead to developing procedural frames within which the EU and the concerned jurisdictions could accommodate their concerns and interests (cf. Joerges and Schmid 2011: 293 ff., Azoulai 2013).

## The European 'social market economy'

Hence, there are alternatives to the much criticised 'marketisation' of ever more policy fields, even though the search for solutions may be more demanding than abolishing the obstacles to market-building. The dominance of neoliberal strategies requires explanations beyond assertions of an irresistible neoliberal tilt that would have been built into the European project from its inception. As Höpner suggests, it is the increasing socioeconomic diversity and the conflict constellations generated by this diversity that render cooperative problem-solving even more difficult and unlikely (Höpner 2014: 17 ff.). The much criticised judgments in which the ECJ held that the four economic freedoms as conceptualised by European law trump collective labour law and protective national legislation seem to confirm this assumption (CJEU 2007a, b, 2008; cf. CJEU 2014a and Joerges and Rödl 2009).

This jurisprudence affected a core issue of European legitimacy: namely, its commitment to the legacy of the welfare state as reaffirmed in Article 3(3) TEU. Is the EU a 'social market economy'? Can it become one? If not, what are the implications for the legitimacy of the European project and its sustainability?

Answers to these questions require conceptual clarifications. The *soziale Marktwirtschaft* was Germany's post-war social model, on which ordo-liberal economists and jurists, Christian and Social Democrats, employer organisations, and trade unions had reached consensus. It seems obvious that the EU could not adopt an equivalent to Germany's 'social market economy' as conceptualised in the formative phase of the Federal Republic. The reasons are significant in the present context because the social market economy is a synthesis of economic and social ordering. This synthesis was not entirely harmonious. One solution was found in Walter Eucken's theory of 'interdependent orders' (Eucken 1990: 180 ff.; Wegmann 2002: 369 ff.; Tuori 2010), in which the economic order was restricted to the commodity and service markets and complemented by a set of other orders organised in specific patterns. Thus, for example, the *Arbeitsverfassung* (labour constitution) acknowledged that labour must not be subjected to the regular discipline of markets and should instead profit from a system of industrial relations with strong trade unions; and a *Sozialverfassung* (social constitution) should be organised with social welfare entitlements (Foucault 2008: 159 ff.).

Simultaneously but independently, Alfred Müller-Armack started to develop a 'theory of the social market economy' (Müller-Armack 1947, 1966b; cf. Glossner 2010: 47 ff.). Though Müller-Armack often underlined the compatibility of his concepts with ordo-liberal principles, his pleas for a state-provided 'system of social and societal measures' (Müller-Armack 1966a, 1966b) were not entirely in line with the views of the ordo-liberal Minister for the Economy Ludwig Erhard, who posited that a strong antitrust law would be the best conceivable social policy (Abelshauser 2004: 190). This tension is significant: The relation between 'the economic' and 'the social' was not written in stone, but continuously rebalanced and reconfigured (Joerges and Rödl 2004). It makes a difference whether the body politic in which these processes occur has comprehensive legislative competences or is instead entrusted to different levels of governance.

Taking this from the case of Germany to that of the EU, the interdependence of economic, labour, and social policy is due to the lack of pertinent European competences, which again leads to diagonal conflict constellations between levels of governance. The parallels between this situation and that of the EMU are also striking with regard to the EU's means to deal with these tensions. Such means are limited and mostly 'soft': For example, the overriding commitment to a 'competitive social market economy' (Article 3(3) TEU) is but a vague restatement of the problem. The Charter of Fundamental Rights of the European Union cannot fill the Union's social lacunae. To be sure, the Community Charter of the Fundamental Social Rights of Workers was ratified by the Treaty of Lisbon (Article 6 TEU), but in order to become effective, social rights need to be substantiated in special legislation, which may require competences beyond the EU's powers. They also require a broader political legitimacy than the judiciary can generate on its own. Furthermore, the Open Method of Coordination on which many hopes had been pinned (Trubek and Trubek 2005; Dawson 2011) has not been constitutionalised, and the type of coordination provided for in Articles 5.1, 5.2, and 156 TFEU provides no functional equivalent (Braams 2013: 229 ff.; Dawson 2011: 164 ff.). The decoupling of the process of economic integration from the welfare state that Scharpf diagnosed (2002, 2010) has not been overcome (Joerges 2009; Rödl 2013).

### An interim remark

We have to conclude that two of the Habermasian cornerstones upon which the legitimacy of constitutional democracy depends–namely, the primacy of democratic legitimacy over economic governance and a viable commitment to social justice–cannot be ensured within the institutional framework of the EU as it stands. The reliance on law in the integration project has only furthered, rather than prevented, the erosion of its legitimacy. According to one view that is even more widely shared after the height of the economic crisis, Europe is bound to strive for deeper integration in order to overcome its impasses, although it seems far from clear how such a process might be initiated successfully, and its *finalité* remains opaque. The concluding section will discuss the prevailing version of the 'more Europe' thesis and question its adequacy.

## The European Trilemma

To-day, it is easy enough to see past mistakes. But it is much less easy to undo their consequences' (Polanyi 1937: preface 9). This observation referred to the Great Depression. History does not repeat itself: We see past mistakes, but our errors today are distinct. Our understanding of the present draws on a broader knowledge basis, and our potential to react looks much better, not least because so many activities are organised transnationally. Seemingly paradoxically, however, the expansion of knowledge and the strengthening of transnational ties neither provide safe theoretical guidance nor ensure reliable transnational political coordination and action.

As Krastev has put it, 'Europe finds itself squeezed between the impotence of national politics, the democratic deficit of European policies and the growing mistrust of the markets' (Krastev 2012: 1), summarising the threefold challenge facing Europe. The complex interdependencies of the three problems exceed not only the potential of deliberate policy-making but also the conceptual capabilities of political actors and advisors. Our awareness of political processes, economic constraints, and normative debates cannot be synthesised. The disciplines involved in the exploration of the causes of the crisis, the development of governance strategies, and the assessment of their efficacy operate under uncertainties and cannot rule out that analyses will prove deficient and that recommendations will generate new risks. The law cannot fill the lacunae of economic knowledge and must not anticipate the outcome of political processes. Its vocation is rather to ensure through procedural safeguards the normative quality of responses to uncertainties and of political contestation (cf. Habermas 1996: 427 ff.).

The concluding section of this chapter seeks to accomplish this through the juxtaposition of 'normalisation' and 'contestation'. Here, 'normalisation' denotes a readiness to accept the new realities of crisis governance, whereas 'contestation' denotes a search for a renewed constitutional condition. Our resort to 'contestation' is a normative choice that builds upon the concept of 'conflicts-law constitutionalism'. This section first sketches the approach before turning to a critique of the new modes of European crisis management and finally an elaboration of the choice between normalisation and contestation.

## The conflicts-law approach in a nutshell

The conflicts-law approach is an alternative to the orthodoxy of European law as petrified under the impact of the integration-through-law project (Joerges 2014c; Joerges, Kjaer, and Ralli 2011). This approach refrains from conceptualising European law as an ever growing and more comprehensive body of rules and principles of progressively richer normative qualities. After enlargement and in view of deepening socio-economic heterogeneity, European law must learn instead to live with the varieties of its capitalism. It has to take the fortunate motto presented in Article I-8 of the otherwise unfortunate draft 2003 Constitutional Treaty seriously. 'United in diversity' should be understood as Europe's true vocation, and–this is the jurisprudential gist of the approach–its vocation can be realised through a new type of conflicts law understood as Europe's constitutional form. While this proposition has its technical complexities, its core analytical assumptions and normative messages can be simply restated.

In essence, EU member states are no longer autonomous. They are in many ways interdependent and hence depend upon cooperation. This cooperation, however, is unlikely to lead to the establishment of a strong federal entity in the foreseeable future. In view of the histories of European democracies and their uneven potential and willingness to pursue the same objectives of distributional justice, respond consistently to economic and financial instabilities, and cope uniformly with environmental challenges, it is unlikely that Europeans will converge in their political perspectives, that the institutional varieties of European forms of capitalism and economic cultures will disappear, or that, considering the enormous complexity of their social systems and the diversity of their entitlements, they will institutionalise a uniform pan-European welfare system (cf. Manow 2001b; Abelshauser 2013). The sustainability of the European project seems to depend upon the construction and institutionalisation of a third alternative between or beyond the defence of the nation state, on the one hand, and federalist ambitions, on the other. Recent varieties of capitalism analyses of the impacts of the eurozone crisis document the resistance of the institutional configuration and the European economies against command-and-control changes; their findings cast doubt on the assumption that the destruction of this configuration would generate some superior alternative. Expectations of crisis management and austerity politics may be that the member states in difficulties will move towards the Anglo-Saxon type of liberal capitalism, but it is difficult to predict whether this will happen and how it might improve competitive conditions.

The idea of a European conflicts law conceptualises the implications of these observations in legal terms. The first concerns a dilemma of democratic will-formation. Constitutional states are increasingly unable to guarantee the inclusion of all who are impacted by their policies and the politics of internal decision-making processes, yet the democratic notion of self-legislation, which postulates that the addressees of a law should be able to understand themselves as its authors, demands 'the inclusion of the other'.

As a consequence of their interdependence, EU member states are therefore no longer in a position to guarantee the democratic legitimacy of their policies. A European law that concerns itself with the amelioration of such external effects (i.e. that seeks to compensate for the democratic shortcomings of national decision-making processes) may induce its legitimacy from this function. With this, European law can free itself from the critique of its legitimacy, which has accompanied it since its founding. Instead of asking the EU to correct its democracy deficit, we should develop the potential for European law to compensate for the structural democracy deficits of its member states (cf. Innerarity forthcoming).

Three challenges that are of particular importance for the evaluation of Europe's crisis management follow from these premises. The first concerns the definition of the undemocratic external impact of national decision-making and the delineation of what it might take to compensate for it through European law. The second concerns the definition and establishment of cooperative arrangements and procedures that 'deserve recognition'. The third relates to the handling of 'true' conflict constellations (i.e. those in which a positive solution cannot be achieved and in which undecidability might be the result) (Lenoble 1996; for a European example cf. Joerges 2013).

## Crisis governance

As argued above, the fragility of the Maastricht arrangement was a birth defect that remained hidden until the economic crisis began to unfold in 2008. Since then, we have witnessed the turbo-speed proliferation of new modes of EU economic governance and regulatory mechanisms, most of which have been discussed in previous chapters of this Report.

Three features of the new modes and mechanisms of economic governance seem particularly intriguing in light of the legitimacy *problématique* and the legitimacy-mediating function of European law. First, through the supervision and control of macroeconomic imbalances, Europe's praxis disregards the principle of enumerated powers and competences and cannot respect the democratic legitimacy of national institutions, in particular the budgetary powers of the parliaments of those states receiving assistance. Second, the departure from the 'one-size-fits-all' philosophy, observed for example in the European Semester (cf. Chapter 3), so far fails to achieve a variation that might be based on democratically legitimated choices. To the contrary, the individualised scrutiny of all member states is geared to the objective of budgetary balances and seeks to impose the necessary discipline. Under the conditions of a monetary union, member states can only respond to pertinent requests through austerity measures: reductions of wage levels and social entitlements (cf. Dawson and de Witte 2013: 825-7). Third, the machinery of the new regime, with individualised measures oriented only by indeterminate general clauses, is regulatory in nature and establishes a transnational executive apparatus outside the realm of democratic politics and the accountability previously guaranteed by the rule of law. This type of de-legalisation is accompanied by assessments of member state performance that cannot be anything but highly discretionary (Everson 2013, forthcoming).

As noted, the legacy of the welfare state is an essential dimension of the legitimacy of the European project. That commitment is seriously at risk. Under the Euro Plus Pact and Article 1 of the Treaty on Stability, Coordination and Governance (TSGC), fostering competitiveness in the eurozone has become the new primary concern of economic governance. According to Article 1 TSGC, 'sustainable growth, employment and social cohesion' remain European objectives. However, in such important documents as the 'Blueprint for a Deep and Genuine Economic and Monetary Union: Launching a European Debate' (European Commission 2012), the 'European social model' is no longer on the agenda; the means to foster competitiveness are 'structural reforms' in 'member states in difficulties', and these reforms are primarily austerity measures (Deakin 2014: 101 ff.).

> *The legacy of the welfare state is an essential dimension of the legitimacy of the European project.*

Has this reconceptualisation of European governance been inspired by German ordo-liberalism, as many critics argue (Dullien and Guérot 2012)? Such assignments of conceptual responsibility disregard the reservations of leading scholars committed to the ordo-liberal tradition and its concepts of *Ordnungspolitik*. The Maastricht promise of a stability union, they submit, was not institutionalised by adequate incentive structures (cf. Feld 2011); a sustainable implementation of conditionality was inconceivable (cf. Konrad

2013). Kurt Biedenkopf, a passionate ordo-liberal in academia and politics (cf. Biedenkopf 2012), even accused former German Chancellor Kohl of having programmed a disaster when agreeing to the common currency (Böll 2011). What is furthermore disregarded is the *proprium* of the ordo-liberal tradition, namely its synthesis of law and economics and the implication that economic policy must be guided by law and justiciable criteria (Mestmäcker 1973; Vanberg 2014). Be that as it may, the situational, largely discretionary interventionism through the executive and governmental bodies is anathema to ordo-liberal scholarship. As explained earlier, the Maastricht EMU has instituted an unruly conflict that could not be managed within the institutional frameworks of the EMU and the SGP. The ECB had to step in and exercise precisely the type of discretion which ordo-liberalism rejected. To cite again the opinion delivered by Cruz Villalòn (CJEU 2015). 'The ECB must ... be afforded a broad discretion for the purpose of framing and implementing the Union's monetary policy ... Therefore, the intensity of judicial review of the ECB's activity ... must be characterised by a considerable degree of caution' (para. 111).

What is so ordo-liberal about a project and a praxis that the leading protagonists of the ordo-liberal tradition reject? We also have to ask: If the new economic governance is not an ordo-liberal project, how else should it be characterised? The list of suggestions is long: 'new sovereignty with largely unfettered power of rule' (Chalmers 2013: 1); 'decision-making that eschew forms of electoral accountability and popular democratic control' (Curtin 2014: 205); '*postdemokratischer Exekutivföderalismus*' (post-democratic executive federalism) (Habermas 2011); 'authoritarian managerialism' (Joerges and Weimer 2013; Joerges 2014b); a move from 'democratic deficit' to 'democratic default' (Majone 2014: 179 ff.); 'a legally and politically unconstrained expert regime' (Scharpf 2013: 12); 'consolidating state' (Streeck 2013: 16 ff.); 'authoritarian liberalism' (Wilkinson 2014: 23). Furthermore, in Chapter 3, Dawson calls the new type of governance a 'coordinative method', adding that 'the level of sovereignty a state enjoys increasingly depends on its solvency'. 'Executive mode' (*Exekutivmodus*) is the term Henrik Enderlein used in an earlier publication (Enderlein 2013: 722 f.).

All of these notions signal discontent with the present European praxis. None fail to consider the pressures and constraints under which Europe's crisis management operates. These measures were taken to compensate for the failure of the original EMU and Stability and Growth Pact and sought to prevent the collapse of the eurozone's financial system. If they cannot be understood as some wilful, let alone malicious, disregard of legal rules and principles, then how?

Already in 2010, Böckenförde, former judge of the German Constitutional Court, started to talk of a state of emergency (Böckenförde 2010), a notion he had earlier defined as a breakdown of the correlation between the regular situation presupposed in the law as the reference point of its regulatory objectives (Böckenförde 1978: 1884). This breakdown generates a discrepancy and tension between conferred powers and means, on the one hand, and irrefutable challenges of a state of emergency, on the other (1978: 1885). In such exceptional circumstances, Böckenförde submitted, we will observe the quest for exceptional powers and means to cope with such emergencies. Such explanations seem to capture the exigencies of the present crisis quite well (Scheuerman 2000; Dyson 2013; White 2013). If we have to concede that the establishment of the EMU was a mistake that cannot be corrected by a stricter enforcement of its rules, the resort to exceptional measures after the collapse of this fragile edifice is unsurprising. But what then?

## Regaining legitimacy

Europe's only alternative to normalisation of its precarious new modes of economic governance is–according to the prevailing view in academic quarters and among political leaders–a move towards stronger European powers with supranational political institutions that are representative and accountable. Economist Dani Rodrik, for example, cites the 'trilemma thesis' (Rodrik 2011: 184-206), asserting the impossibility of the simultaneous pursuit of economic globalisation, democratic politics, and national self-determination and highlighting that only two goals can be paired at one time: economic globalisation and democratic politics, or democracy and national autonomy. According to Rodrik (2014) the EU is a dramatic illustration of this trilemma. The EU could transnationalise democracy through federalisation and thereby defend the advantages of the common market. Federalisation would imply that the EU would also be forced to establish common European politics to legitimise the necessary assumption of fiscal and social policy, with negative consequences for national sovereignty. In the absence of such a de-nationalising will, Rodrik asserts, the EU will have to give up the common currency and accept economic disintegration.

Given the lack of prospects for fast political transformation, the 'stark' choice between federalisation and disintegration with which Rodrik (2014: 5 f.) confronts Europe is purely hypothetical. Modern societies and the EU in particular are much too complex to change in one big bang.

'Exploratory governance' as outlined in Chapter 1 is a third way which acknowledges that insight while insisting that change, even if incremental, has to occur. If 'normalisation' (i.e. accepting the new modes and mechanisms as Europe's new *Verfassungswirklichkeit*, its modes of governance as its constitutional reality) is not a viable option, as scholars such as Innerarity (forthcoming), Weale (forthcoming) and Bach (forthcoming) have agreed, change is at the same time a normative necessity. Exploratory governance is then to be understood as a process of discovery and construction of Europe's future, which must not and cannot be prescribed 'through law' in substance. Law may nevertheless operate as a catalyst in such renewal processes. Its opportunities and challenging tasks are already becoming visible to some degree: They will have little to do with more legal harmonisation but will instead arise in contestation over the conflict configurations being generated by the crisis. The room for political manoeuvre may thereby widen. Such conflict scenarios seem likely.

### *Parliaments and national budgets*

Parliaments were, as many commenters have observed, the great 'losers' in this time of emergency (Benz 2013; Maurer 2013; Neyer 2014). This is true for the European Parliament (EP) as well as for national parliaments such as the German Bundestag (Hassemer 2012). It is by the same token unsurprising, because in emergency situations there is simply no time for deliberation and extensive public debate. But parliaments are also democratic institutions with considerable informal powers. The EP, in a Resolution of 13 March 2014, commented very critically on the role and operations of the Troika (the ECB, Commission, and the International Monetary Fund (IMF)) with regard to the eurozone programme countries (European Parliament 2014). The refusal of France and Italy to comply with budgetary recommendations from Brussels has not yet been framed as a legal conflict but could be in the future.

### *National constitutional courts*

The legal dimension of European responses to the crisis is clear in the jurisprudence of the German Constitutional Court. In its judgment of 7 September 2011 on the Greece bailout (BVerfGE 2011), the German Court underlined that the Bundestag must remain 'the place in which autonomous decisions on revenue and expenditure are made, even with regard to international and European commitments' (para 124), explaining that 'by virtue of its approval of stability aids, the Bundestag exercises the influence demanded by the Constitution and is a participant in decisions on the amount, conditionality and length of stability aids. It therefore determines the most important conditions for future successful demands for capital disbursements under Article 9(2) ESM Treaty' (para 274).

This has been praised as a confirmation of a democratic essential, but the Court's statement is deeply problematic. For one, the control that the Bundestag can exercise exists only on paper (Hassemer 2012). Even more troubling are its normative flaws. The German Court endorses the practice of 'strict conditionality' without even considering that practice's compatibility with European commitments to democracy and the rule of law. Compliance with those commitments is not just a supranational command. Respect for the common constitutional principles of EU member states must be understood as a command of European, international, and German constitutional law. At stake is the core premise of conflicts-law constitutionalism. Constitutional democracies, in particular EU member states, have to understand that democratic governance is conceivable only cooperatively and requires the 'recognition of the other' (Dawson and de Witte 2013: 825-7). How then can the German Constitutional Court ensure that its holdings will protect the democratic rights of its citizens? Germany and its citizens are part of a Union of equals. Budgetary autonomy is a common European constitutional legacy, respect for which is demanded by Article 4(2) TEU.

There is a parallel here to the relations between national parliaments. Just as parliaments must recognise each other, constitutional courts in the EU must be prepared to enter into judicial dialogues (Viellechner 2012; Wendel 2013). They could thereby flesh out the limits of executive surveillance of their powers (see Chapter 3 of this Report).

*Cooperative problem-solving*

The interaction of parliaments and the dialogue of courts as envisaged here assume that EU member states are equals, compelled to respect the fundamental rights of all European citizens and their democratic institutions. 'Strict conditionality' of financial aid (Art. 136(3) TFEU) is irreconcilable with these principles if exercised one-sidedly in authoritarian ways. However, that need not be so. Discussions on fiscal policy, macroeconomic imbalances, financial sector issues, and growth-enhancing structural reforms in the context of the European Semester (see Figure 3.1) are only conceivable as interactive processes. This assumption is confirmed by analyses that underline that the effective coordination of macroeconomic policies presupposes cooperation and must accept in principle national ownership of the Semester process (Marzinotto, Wolff, and Hallerberg 2012). Again, factual insights and normative principles point in the same direction. Conditionality can work only if actors agree upon objectives and pursue them cooperatively, hence transforming command and control concepts of conditionality into processes of cooperative problem-solving.

*Defending social rights*

While in all of these contexts a civilising impact of law on Europe's crisis management can be expected with some confidence–perhaps even leading to some policy innovations–such prospects are difficult to discern with regard to the hard core of so-called structural reforms. There is protest in many 'countries in difficulties' but hardly any counter-movement with an elaborated strategy. National trade unions and the European Trade Union Institute continue to produce studies that register cuts in the minimum wage, the weakening of sector-level collective agreements, and the promotion of temporary and fixed-term employment at the expense of permanent jobs. Even they must realise that the diversity of European economic conditions, institutional configurations, and policy orientations renders the development of transnational action plans extremely difficult. Pertinent studies explore mainly the potential of law to defend human rights and social entitlements against the implementation of austerity politics at the national level (cf. Fischer-Lescano 2014). There is so far not much to report. One signal, however, has been sent by Portugal's Constitutional Court (Tribunal Constitucional Portugal 2013), which has examined the compatibility of the Portuguese government's austerity measures with the Portuguese Constitution. The Court explicitly recognised 'the seriousness of the current economic/financial situation and the need to attain the public-deficit goals included in the specific economic policy conditions laid down in the memoranda of understanding between the Portuguese government, the European Union and the International Monetary Fund'. However, it then objected to the implementation of these requests because of their disregard for the principles of equality and proportionality. As underlined in Chapter 3 of this Report, the positions of the German Constitutional Court, which defends conditionality in the interest of Germany's budgetary risks, and the reservations of Portugal's Constitutional Court are asymmetric (cf. Wilkinson 2014). It is precisely this type of undemocratic external effect of solipsistic national decision-making that, according to the concept of conflicts-law constitutionalism, European law should supervise and compensate. The tragic irony of Europe's 'crisis law' is that it provides for measures that are irreconcilable with the normative legacy of the European project.

*Distributional conflicts*

The most sensitive conflicts are distributional and can be observed within and between European societies (Bach forthcoming; Streeck and Elsässer 2014). As is the case with defending social rights, these conflicts have provoked social unrest but hardly anything like organised social movements with a constructive political agenda. Seemingly paradoxically, the most powerful organiser of distributional politics is now the ECB, another excellent example of a non-majoritarian institution. Redistribution occurs as collateral damage or benefit through the Bank's extensive understanding of monetary policy, most notably through the OMT programme and turn to quantitative easing. Equally paradoxically, two other non-majoritarian institutions are involved in the contest over the OMT programme, namely the German Constitutional Court (BVerfGE 2014) and the CJEU. The contest can be observed, but the conflict cannot be resolved as has been explained above (also Joerges 2014a: 785). There is no law under which the conflict about the assignment of powers over monetary and economic policy could be decided and the proper scope of these policies legally defined.

## Epilogue: 'Wo aber Gefahr ist, wächst das Rettende auch'

The European integration process has relied on a broad consensus among member states and their citizens, with progress achieved through compromise. The analyses of the conflict constellations that need to be addressed and the suggestion that contestation is unavoidable imply that this might lead to more diversity and differentiation. Obviously this is at odds with recent efforts to strengthen economic convergence. These efforts may indeed strengthen the common currency, but one can never be sure.

The varieties of capitalism school (Iversen and Soskice 2013; Hall 2014) indicates that the institutional configurations of European capitalism have neither been affected in their substance nor found ways to defend their essentials in processes of adaptation (Manow 2001b). The findings of economic historians confirm that stability (Abelshauser 2013; Abelshauser, Gilgen, and Leutzsch 2012), as do sociologically informed inquiries into the functioning of national and transnational markets (Ladeur 2014; Teubner 2014). These kinds of obstacles militate against the reasonableness of command and control convergence policies. Werner Abelshauser even submits that the co-existence of different economic cultures is not only possible but productive and beneficial (Abelshauser 2014: 19 f.). Hall (2014: 1239) concurs: 'National distinctiveness was not seen as inimical to international solidarity. The motto of the EU is not "uniformity" but, rather, "unity in diversity"–and the future of European integration will depend on Europe's capacity to give substance to that slogan'.

'Conflicts-law constitutionalism' was a project that understood unity in diversity as Europe's vocation and conflicts law as its legal form (Joerges 2014c). The crisis may have damaged the reconstructive status of that project, but not its normative credentials and perhaps not even its economic sociological assumptions.

**Endnotes**

1. 'Wealth maximisation is no substitute for the purpose of law in general' (Mestmäcker 2007). This one sentence illuminates the discrepancy between the Hayekian and the Chicago version of economic liberalism well enough.

2. On the intense controversies in Germany over the common currency at the time of its introduction, see Heinemann (2013).

# V. Governance Indicators

LIAM F. MCGRATH

## Introduction

The eurozone crisis has led to increased attention to governance issues within the European Union. A number of countries have faced severely negative economic conditions as a result of the crisis, and this economic decline has been coupled with record low levels of trust in various EU institutions such as the European Parliament (EP), as well as in the EU itself.

As noted in Chapter 2, problems caused by further integration when divergence exists between countries are a key issue for the EU. In institutional frameworks that require homogeneity to work effectively, such as Europe's economic and monetary union (EMU)[1], existing divergence in outcomes can be reinforced and exacerbated, as well as lead to negative outcomes for particular countries or groups of countries. In addition, divergence in outcomes often leads to divergence in the policy preferences of governments, which makes future institutional changes aimed at improving governance more difficult to implement.

> *Divergence in outcomes often leads to divergence in the policy preferences of governments, which makes future institutional changes more difficult to implement.*

The indicator suite developed for *The Governance Report 2015* contains a wide array of macroeconomic outcome variables as well as measures of aggregate public opinion for countries within the EU. The indicators allow us to conduct a variety of analyses that help describe whether EU countries have been moving closer together or further apart in particular ways over the last 15 years. Furthermore, these indicators allow us to see whether convergence or divergence has been more pronounced within clusters of countries, or so-called 'convergence clubs', within the EU. As a result, we are able to better understand the extent to which governance challenges related to divergence are widespread throughout the EU or more pronounced within specific groups of countries. Nonetheless, it should be kept in mind that although progress may be made in convergence, this does not imply that important differentials do not still exist between countries.

In addition to these convergence indicators, we also provide indicators that measure associations between macroeconomic trends and aggregate public opinion. Such indicators permit exploration of, for example, whether negative economic outcomes entail declining trust in EU institutions by examining past associations between these outcomes. As in the case of our convergence indicators, we also allow disaggregation of these trends into specific groups of countries, as well as distinct time periods, to determine whether there are cases in which these challenges to governance are most acute. In doing so, we can better comprehend issues of legitimacy and trust in the EU at such a crucial time.

This approach is in keeping with the governance indicators developed for previous editions of the Governance Report (Hertie School of Governance 2013, 2014). Rather than providing a single number that measures or ranks economic or public opinion convergence over the last few years, we offer a series of disaggregated indicators in the form of a dashboard. Thus, we are able to uncover the nuances of convergence within the EU by addressing questions that cannot be resolved with a single convergence estimate. The indicators allow us to examine whether there are multiple convergence processes occurring simultaneously on a given outcome, whether convergence in some outcomes has been less affected by the financial and fiscal crises than others, and whether some outcomes are converging more rapidly than others, amongst many more questions.

The next section introduces our set of indicators measuring convergence by detailing the methodological approach and providing a sample of analyses using the indicators for macroeconomic outcomes and aggregate public opinion. The third section examines the association between macroeconomic outcomes and aggregate public opinion, with an illustration of the link between unemployment and trust in the EU in reference to experiences during the crisis. The final section explores the implications of these analyses.

## Indicators for Convergence

Our core set of indicators allows us to examine the extent of convergence or divergence over time among EU member countries and along a variety of dimensions. Such measures of convergence are important for understanding governance challenges within the EU. A lack of convergence indicates at least two possible scenarios that are relevant in terms of governance. First, diverging outcomes between countries will necessitate more complex governance strategies to tackle problems arising from increased heterogeneity. Second, divergence can be a warning sign for problems that will need to be addressed by changes in governance structures or processes.

To construct our indicators for convergence, we used the sigma approach (Gilardi 2014). This is a common approach used in studies of convergence, some of which have examined the size of the public sector in the OECD (Bernauer and Achini 2000), environmental outcomes in the EU (Neumayer 2001), and the adoption of environmental policies within the OECD and eastern Europe (Tews, Busch, and Jörgens 2003).

The idea behind the sigma approach is relatively straightforward: If outcomes in countries are converging, then we would expect to see less variation in those outcomes over time. For our calculation of convergence, we estimate the standard deviation of outcomes for all EU countries in a given year.[2] As such, a decrease in standard deviation, i.e. variation, over time is evidence of convergence, whereas an increase in standard deviation suggests that countries are diverging in outcomes.[3]

Figure 5.1 illustrates how a hypothetical convergence process is captured using the sigma approach. As the outcomes for countries depicted by lines move closer to zero over time, the estimate of convergence, i.e. the standard deviation, decreases. Perfect convergence would result in no variation at all between countries.

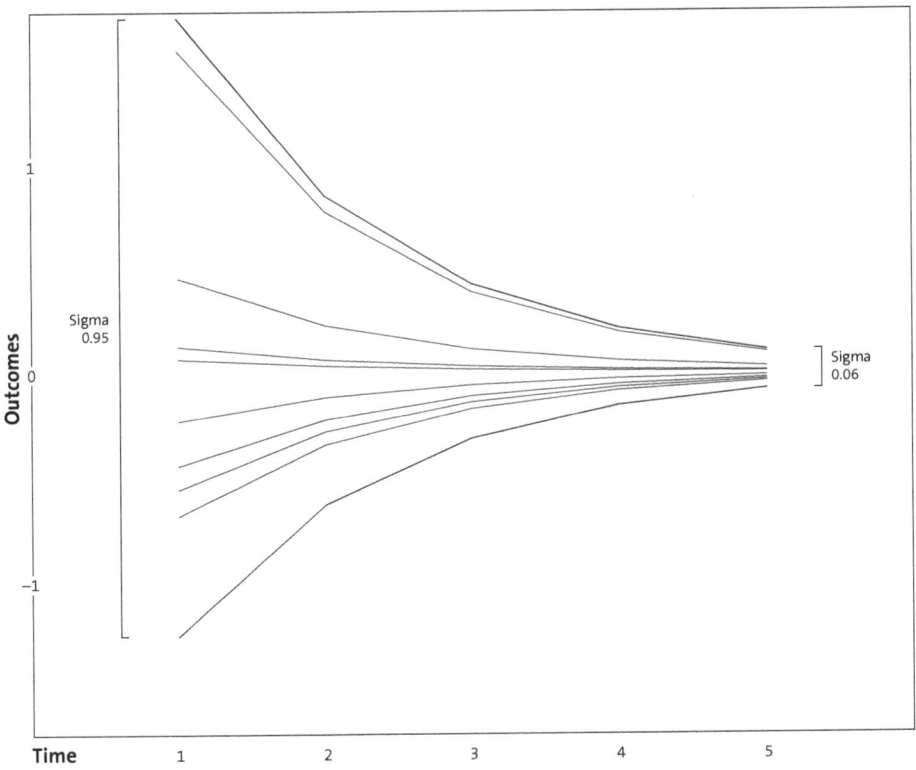

*Figure 5.1* **An example of convergence**

This approach to measuring convergence is not without problems, one of which is the potential to suggest that there is no convergence occuring when there is indeed convergence, albeit of a different form. This occurs when there exist 'convergence clubs' (Plümper and Schneider 2009), subsets of countries that are converging together, although toward a different outcome than that of countries outside the club. Within the EU, for example, there could be a convergence club of eurozone countries and a convergence club of non-eurozone countries. If distinct convergence clubs were converging to different outcomes, then the sigma approach outlined above would indicate that variation was increasing, even though outcomes within the convergence clubs were decreasing in variation. Whilst the measure would still be 'correct' in indicating that variation within the EU was increasing, the issues raised for governance would differ depending on whether eurozone countries were converging to a different point or whether this was a general trend.

Figure 5.2 highlights how a naive sigma approach can imply divergence when in fact there are two distinct groups that are converging to two dif-

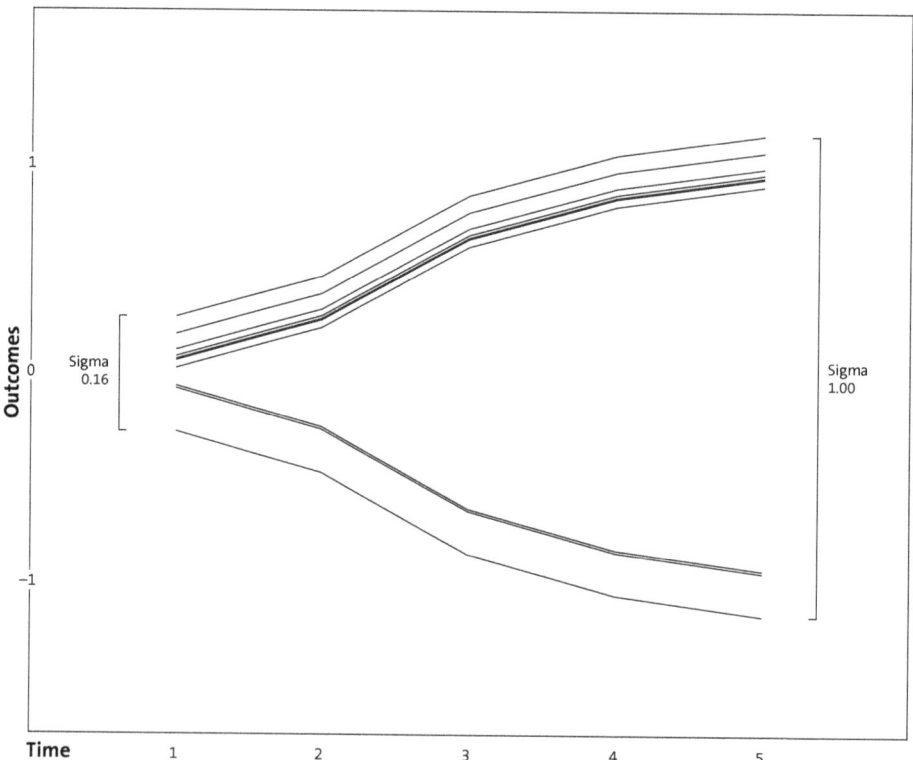

*Figure 5.2* **An example of club convergence**

*Table 5.1* **Subsample of available indicators for convergence**

| Category | Variable | Data Source |
|---|---|---|
| Economic Convergence | Unemployment | Eurostat |
| | Bond Yields | Eurostat |
| | Current Government Expenditure (% GDP) | Eurostat |
| | Net Lending/Borrowing by Government (% GDP) | Eurostat |
| | Exports of Goods and Services (% GDP) | Eurostat |
| | Imports of Goods and Services (% GDP) | Eurostat |
| | Total Government Revenue (% GDP) | Eurostat |
| | Inflation | Eurostat |
| | GDP (per capita) | Eurostat |
| | Gap Between Actual and Trend GDP | Eurostat |
| Public Opinion Convergence | Trust in the EU | Eurobarometer |
| | Trust in the EU Parliament | Eurobarometer |
| | Trust in the National Government | Eurobarometer |
| | Trust in the National Parliament | Eurobarometer |
| | Trust in Political Parties | Eurobarometer |
| | Country Benefits from the Common Market | Eurobarometer |
| | For or Against Economic Monetary Union | Eurobarometer |
| | Satisfaction with Life | Eurobarometer |

ferent outcomes. When simply calculating the convergence statistic for the whole sample, the result suggests that divergence has increased. Whilst this is the case, the divergence is of a particular form: Two convergence clubs are converging on different points and in opposite directions.

In light of this, we have also developed indicators for selected convergence clubs within the EU. This allows for the comparison of convergence trends both between and within different groupings of EU countries and can lend understanding as to whether there may be governance issues for select groups of countries. Many possible convergence clubs can be defined within the EU, e.g. early joiners vs. accession countries, north vs. south, etc., but here we place the focus on original eurozone countries (those 12 countries that joined the euro in the 1999–2001 period) vs. non-eurozone countries.[4]

In keeping with this Report edition's focus on economic and legitimacy challenges currently faced by the EU, we highlight variables that are related to these domains. As the partial listing in Table 5.1 shows, however, our dashboard includes a broad variety of other variables that can be used to generate indicators of convergence.

# Convergence or divergence in economic outcomes within the EU

Given the importance of convergence, or the lack thereof, for understanding governance issues, we now present measures of convergence for selected macroeconomic variables.[5] While there are other variables, such as inflation differentials[6], current account balances, and GDP per capita, that are also considered key to understanding developments in the EMU, we focus on two variables that have particularly drawn the attention of the media and general populace during the current crisis–unemployment rates and bond yields–to illustrate how the indicators serve to highlight patterns. We thereby highlight how our indicators can pick up key issues for governance that have emerged through the crisis. This lends credibility to the indicators as a toolkit for improving our grasp of current issues within the EU and suggests that continuing updates could aid in identifying future issues requiring governance responses.

*Progress in convergence of both bond yields and unemployment rates was dismantled by the financial crisis.*

Figures 5.3 and 5.4 display our indicators of convergence within the EU for unemployment rates and long-term government bond yields, respectively. In the case of unemployment rates (Figure 5.3), there is a clear trend towards convergence in the early 2000s, with variation decreasing by approximately 60 per cent from 2000 to 2007, despite the accession of ten new countries in 2004.[7] A similar pattern is seen for bond yields[8] (Figure 5.4), with the difference in yields declining significantly among the EU member states over that same time period. As clearly shown, progress in convergence of both bond yields and unemployment rates was dismantled by the financial crisis. In both cases, variation within the EU reached levels previously unseen in the last 15 years–three to five times more variation than in 2007.

To ensure that these phenomena are in fact unique to the EU and not simply reflective of global trends, Figure 5.5 calculates the same convergence statistic for unemployment in countries outside the EU.[9] The global unemployment trend clearly differs from that of the EU: Global unemployment rates largely exhibit the same amount of variation over the same time period (consistently having a standard deviation between six and seven percent), with a slight although not statistically significant decrease in the last five years. In the EU, however, the variation ranged between a standard deviation of two percent before the euro crisis and four to six percent in the midst of the crisis. Therefore, the trend of strong pre-crisis convergence followed by strong divergence since the onset of the crisis is somewhat unique to the EU.

But do these patterns hold for the EU as a whole, or are there different convergence processes for different groups of countries within the EU? Figures 5.6 and 5.7 examine the possible existence of convergence clubs within the EU. Here we focus on two of the various potential clubs: the 12 'original' country members of the eurozone, as previously defined, versus those EU countries that are not. Examination of these indicators reveals further information about the divergence in outcomes that has occurred since the financial crisis. For both unemployment rates (Figure 5.6) and bond yields (Figure 5.7), the key driver of our divergence estimate has been the experiences of original eurozone country members. In the pre-crisis period, these countries exhibited greater convergence than other EU countries. However, the onset of the financial crisis led to a dramatic divergence. This is in contrast to the non-eurozone countries, which have also experienced some divergence in outcomes since the beginning of the crisis, although to a much lesser degree. Whilst the variation in outcomes in non-eurozone countries stayed at levels similar to those of the early 2000s, divergence within the eurozone reached levels that had not been seen at all during the euro's existence. As a result, we can expect that issues of governance stemming from diverging country outcomes are most likely to be felt within the eurozone, compared to the rest of the EU.

Our indicators for convergence along selected variables within the EU are complemented by the inspection of time series plots tracing specific countries over time.[10] For example, in order to understand the reasons for the large unemployment rate divergence within the original eurozone countries, a time series plot of unemployment rates for countries in that convergence club can be produced.

Figure 5.8 reveals that the large variation exhibited within the convergence club of original eurozone member countries is mostly a function of the dramatic rise in unemployment in Greece and Spain, as well as in Ireland, Italy, and Portugal to lesser extents. This insight hints at the possible existence of an additional convergence club: those countries impacted most severely by the crisis, or debt crisis countries. This notion is strengthened by looking at Figure 5.9, which presents a time series plot for bond yields. Again a similar picture emerges, with the eurozone debt crisis countries seeing significant increases in bond yields, compared to the relative stability of other eurozone countries.

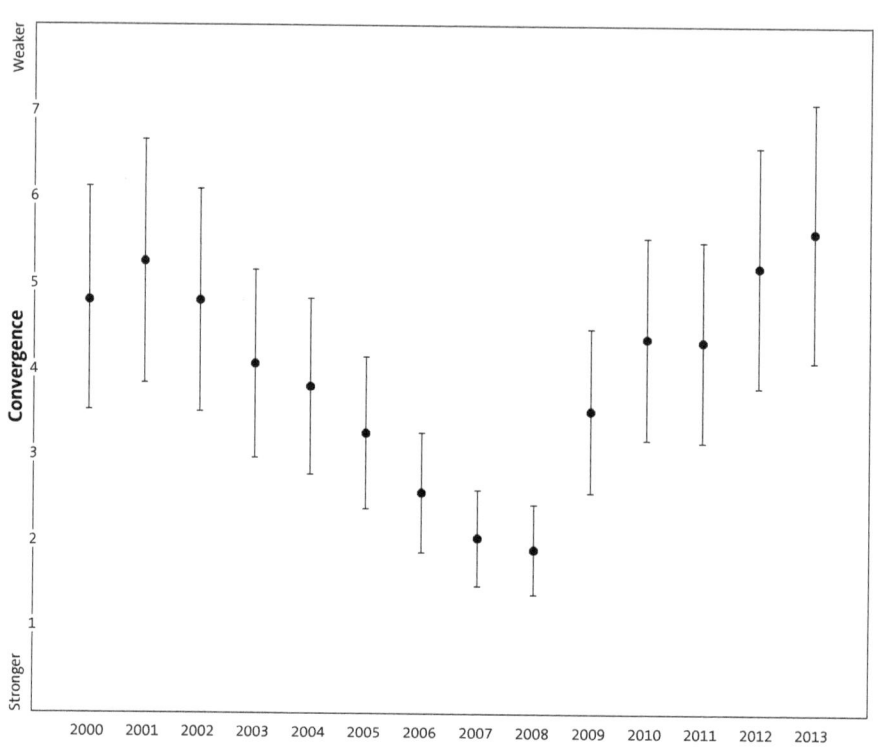

*Figure 5.3* **Convergence in unemployment rates within the EU**

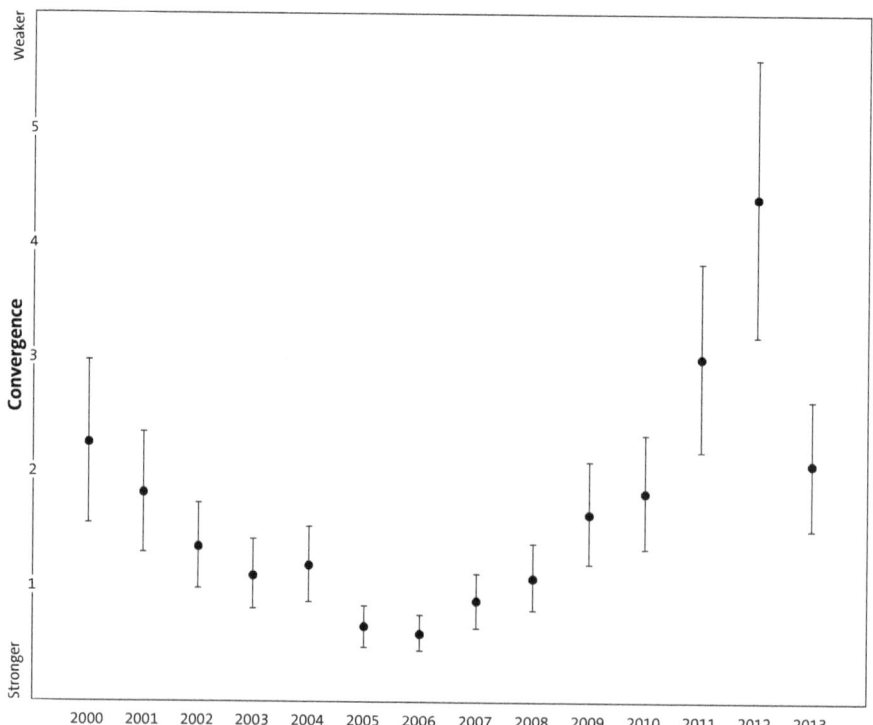

*Figure 5.4* **Convergence in long-term government bond yields within the EU**

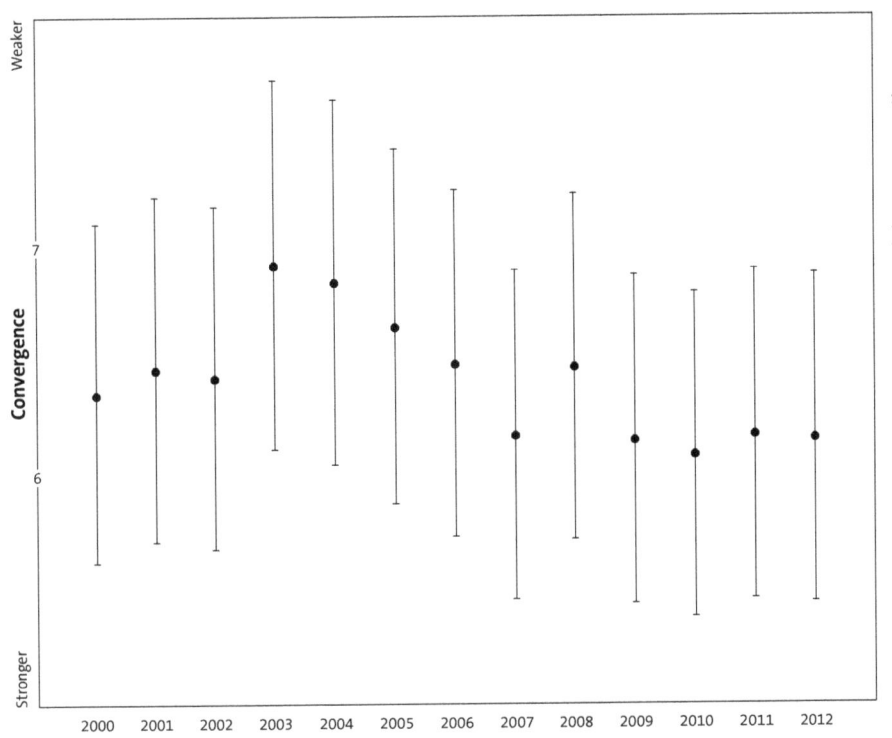

*Figure 5.5* **Convergence in unemployment rates for countries outside the EU**

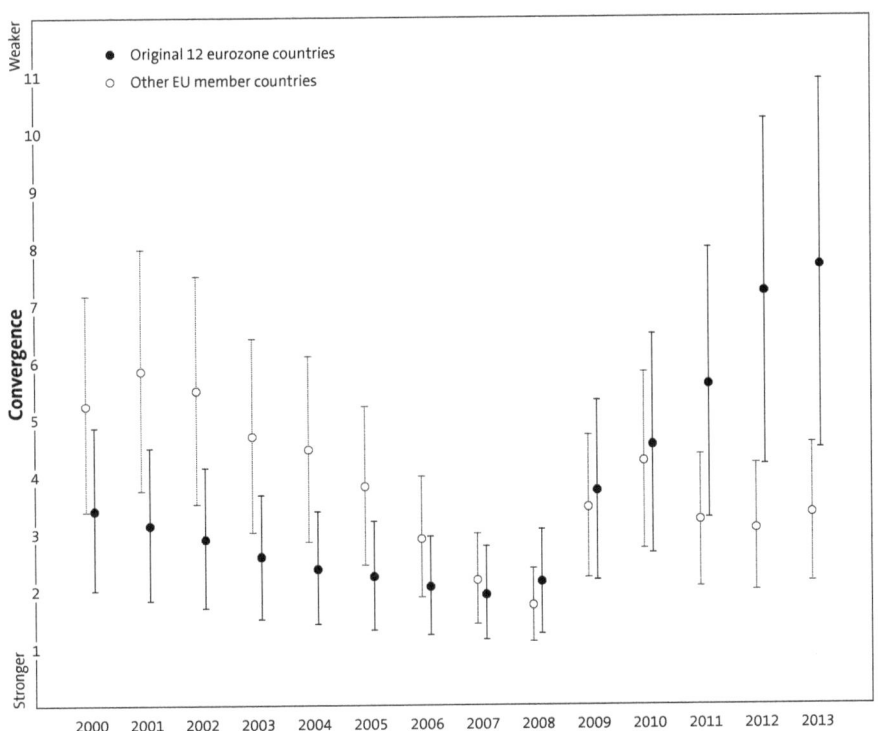

*Figure 5.6* **Convergence in unemployment rates, original eurozone vs. other EU countries**

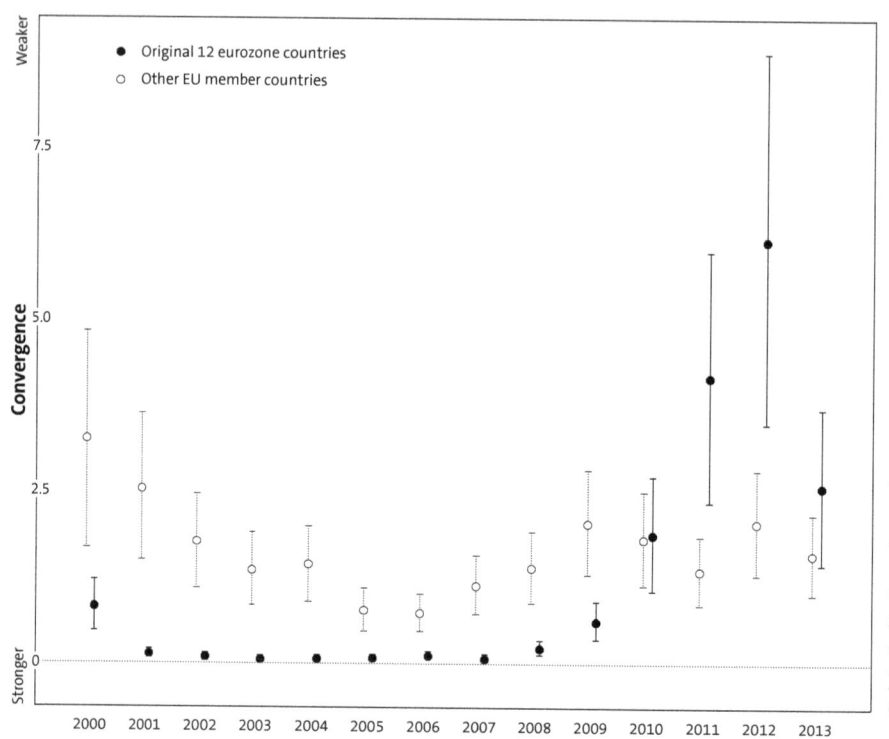

*Figure 5.7* Convergence in bond yields, original eurozone vs. other EU countries

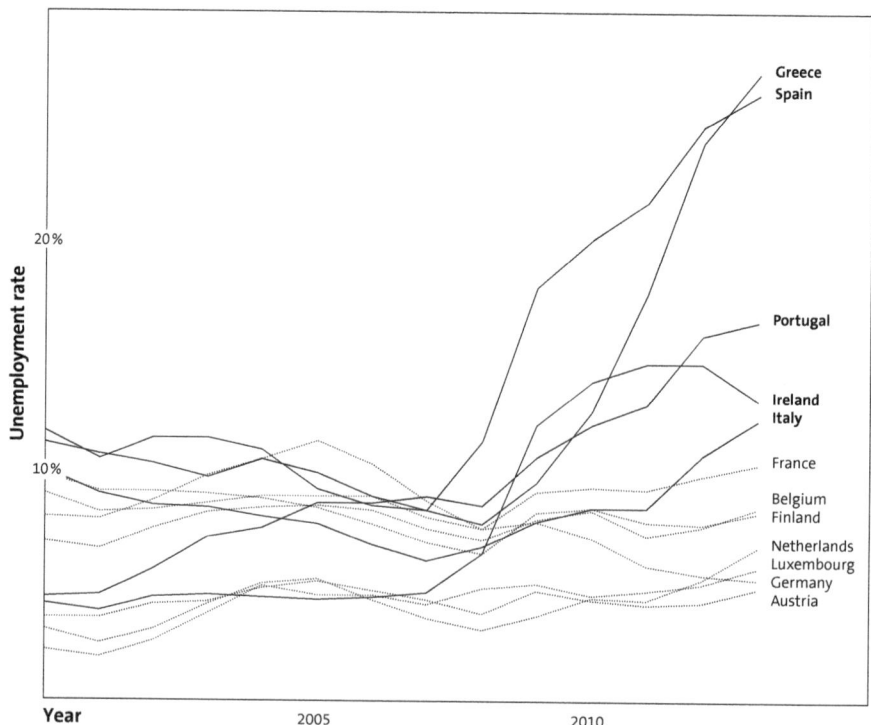

*Figure 5.8* Unemployment rates over time for original eurozone member countries

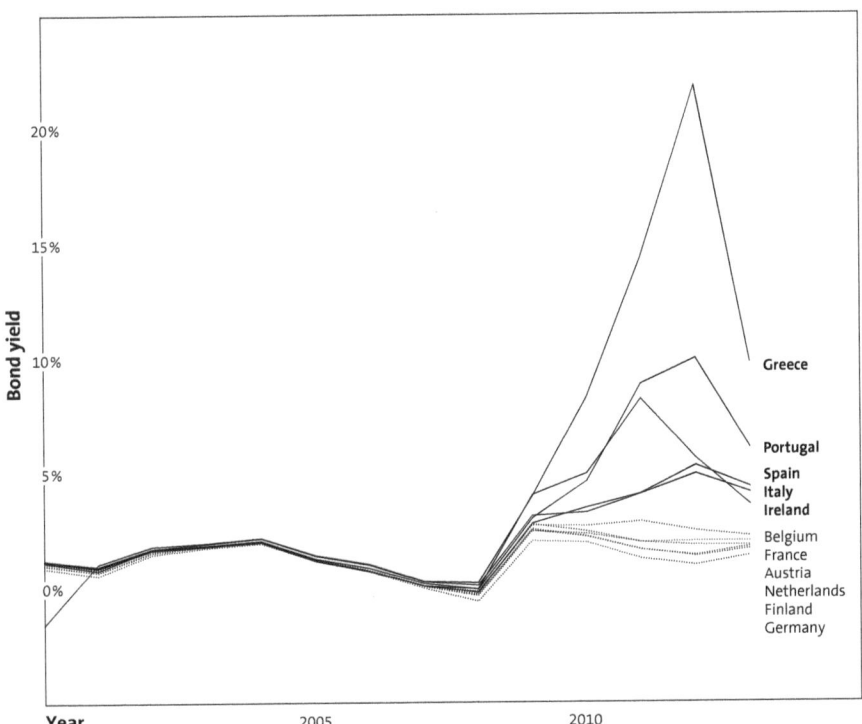

*Figure 5.9* **Bond yields over time for the original eurozone countries**

## Convergence or divergence in public opinion within the EU

By extending our convergence indicator approach to cover trends in public opinion in EU countries, we are able to uncover potential issues for governance related to the legitimacy of and trust in institutions. Such issues pose a different set of challenges than issues pertaining to macroeconomic governance.

As in the previous section, we focus on only a subset of indicators that are available for analysis. In this case, we focus on two important features of public opinion related to the EU. Using data from Eurobarometer (European Commission), we explore first convergence in public opinion relating to trust in the European Parliament (EP) and trust in national parliaments.[11]

As shown in Figures 5.10 and 5.11, which plot the convergence indicators for trust in the European Parliament and in national parliaments, respectively, trust in the European Parliament has remained relatively stable during the last 10 years, with a slight increase in variation in the last few years. On the other hand, as Figure 5.11 illustrates, divergence in trust in national parliaments has risen over the last years, although only modestly.

As in the previous section, we further break down these convergence indicators to account for possible convergence clubs. Figures 5.12 and 5.13

focus again on differences between the 12 original eurozone countries and all other countries in the EU. Similar to the patterns revealed in the macroeconomic convergence section above, those EU countries not in the eurozone are largely stable in their variation in attitudes towards the European and national parliaments. In contrast, among the original eurozone countries, there has been an increasing divergence in public opinion since the onset of the financial crisis. In terms of trust in the European and national parliaments, variation within eurozone countries has increased by approximately 100 per cent since the period directly preceding the crisis.

As before, by producing time series plots of the particular outcome within a given convergence club, we can better understand why the variation among countries has increased so significantly. Depicting eurozone countries with regards to trust in the European Parliament, Figure 5.14 indicates that the large degree of divergence has been driven by incredible collapses in trust within Greece, Portugal, and Spain, as well as within Ireland and Italy to some extent. This is particularly noteworthy as these countries typically had the highest levels of trust in the European Parliament in 2004, yet since the crisis, have experienced the lowest levels of trust.

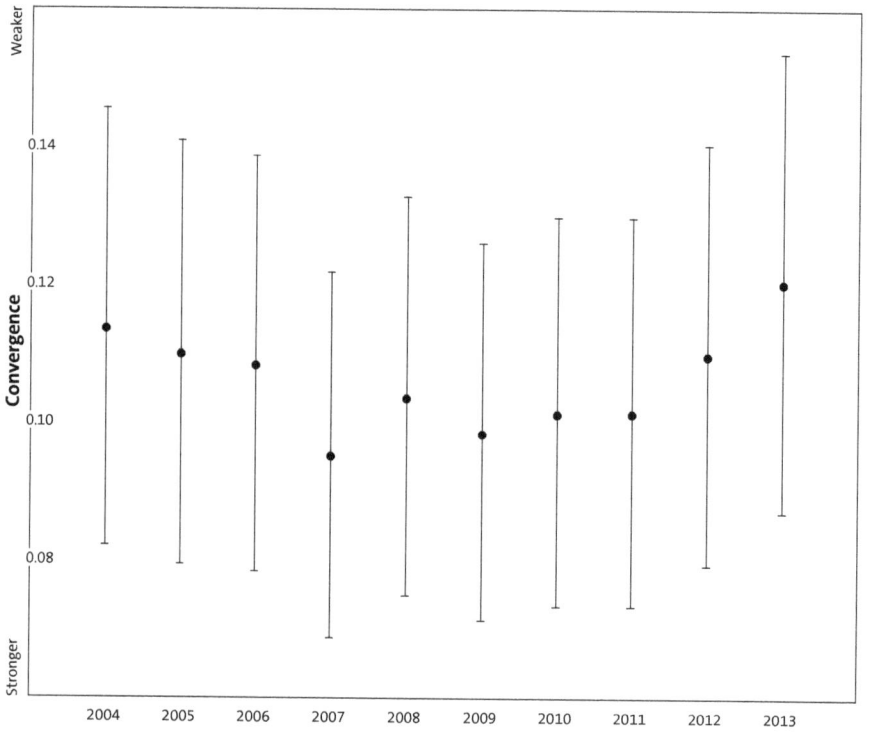

*Figure 5.10* **Convergence in trust in the European Parliament**

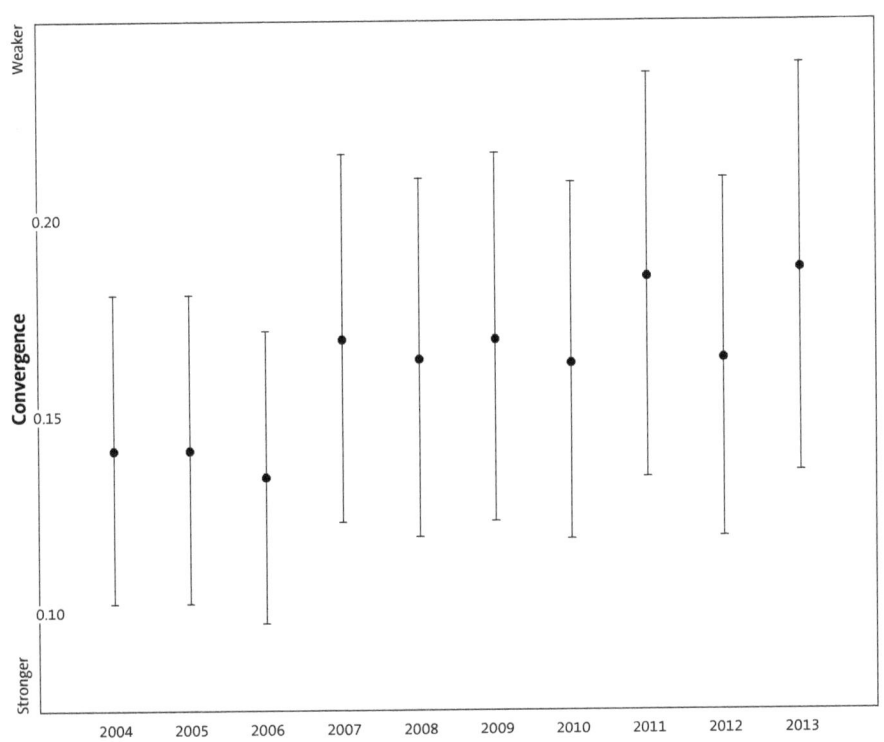

*Figure 5.11* **Convergence in trust in national parliaments**

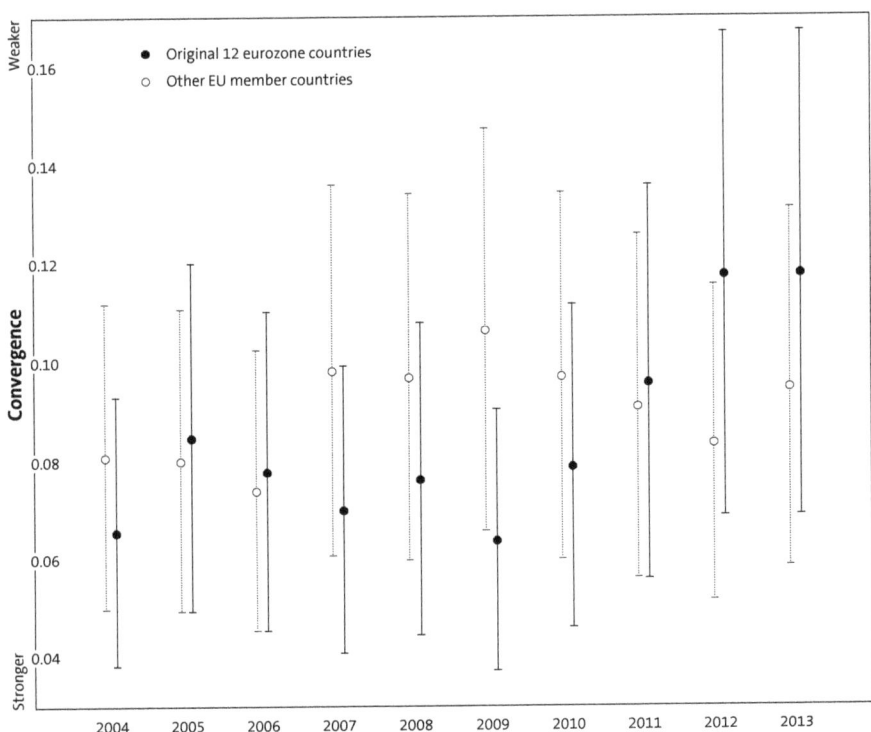

*Figure 5.12* **Convergence in trust in the European Parliament, original eurozone countries vs. other EU countries**

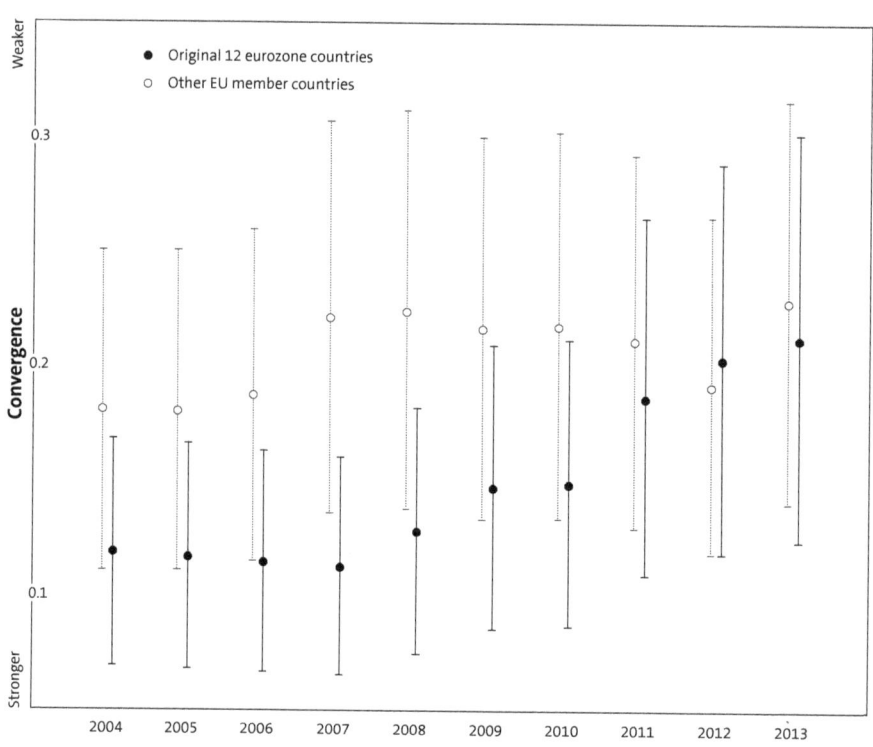

*Figure 5.13* **Convergence in trust in national parliaments, original eurozone countries vs. other EU countries**

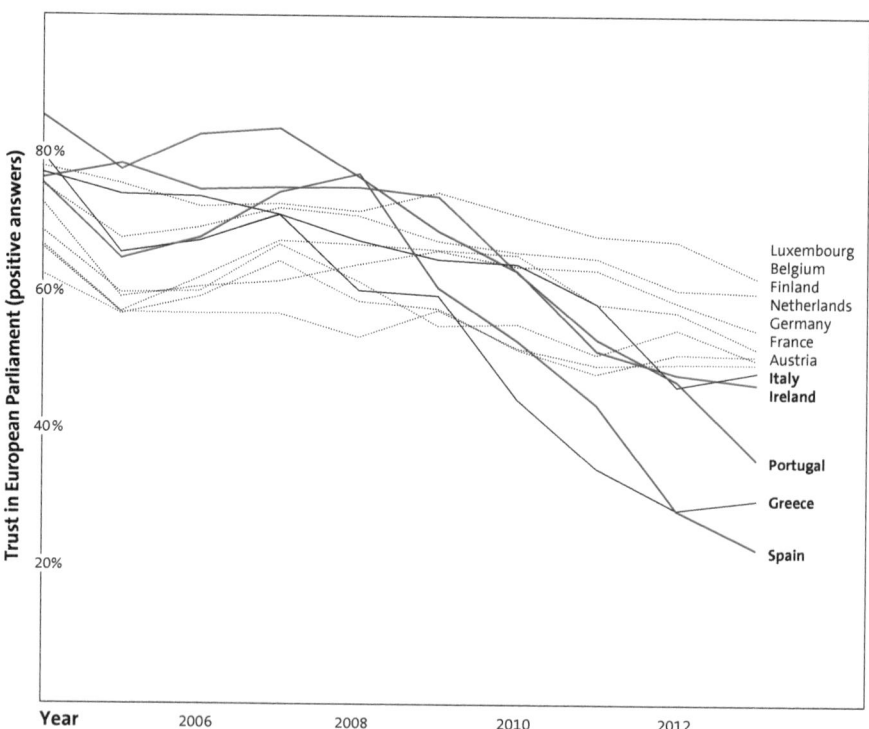

*Figure 5.14* **Trust in the European Parliament over time for the 12 original eurozone countries**

# Aggregate Public Opinion and Economic Conditions

To allow for a deeper understanding of the relationship between macroeconomic outcomes and public opinion in the EU, we developed indicators that record the correlation between the two. This allows for the examination of the possibility of past associations between changing legitimacy and trust in institutions of the EU and its member states in order to identify cases in which changing economic conditions could possibly lead to changing legitimacy and trust in institutions.

Figures 5.15 and 5.16 display the correlation between unemployment and two aggregate trust indicators that focus now on the EU in general and national governments, rather than the respective parliaments. As may be expected, there is a negative association between these indicators in the case of both the EU and national governments. In country-years where there is low unemployment, trust in these institutions is generally higher than in country-years with high unemployment.

The full leverage of our indicators is realised when following a similar disaggregation strategy as in the case of our convergence indicators. In doing so, we may be able to identify differential responsiveness in public opinion to negative trends in economic outcomes, revealing whether there are some cases in which declining economic conditions are not associated with declining trust in institutions, and other cases in which there are strong associations.

As an example, we can focus on the same convergence clubs when examining the relationships between indicators. We can also break down the correlations into specific time periods in order to investigate how these relationships have changed when comparing the period before the financial crisis to the period during the crisis. We therefore gain further leverage on understanding possible challenges for governance that may occur.

To illustrate this, we break the relationship down by comparing the three previously discussed groupings and whether this relationship has changed during the crisis. Figure 5.17 looks at three separate groups: the five debt crisis countries (Greece, Ireland, Italy, Portugal, and Spain), the other seven original country members of the eurozone, and the remaining EU countries.

Notably, the only category in which there is a significant negative relationship between unemployment and trust in the EU is among the five hardest-hit eurozone countries since the crisis began. This potentially indicates an attribution of blame towards the EU by citizens for the deteriorating economic conditions of their countries. In comparison, such a relationship is not seen in non-eurozone countries, whose economic situation has been nonetheless similar to that of the eurozone crisis countries in terms of unemployment. Such a result suggests that as economic and monetary integration deepens within the EU, issues of legitimacy become more pertinent,

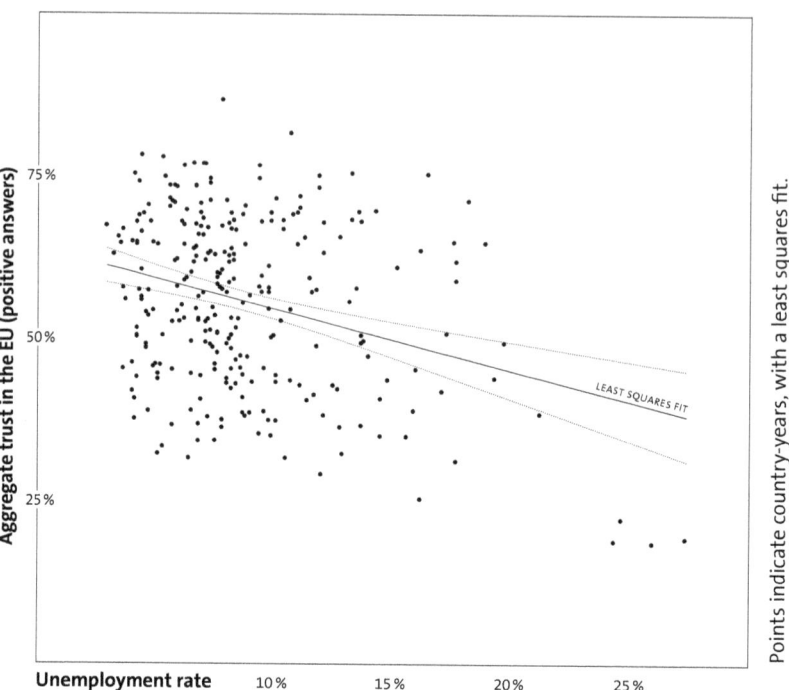

*Figure 5.15* The association between unemployment rates and trust in the EU (2004–2013)

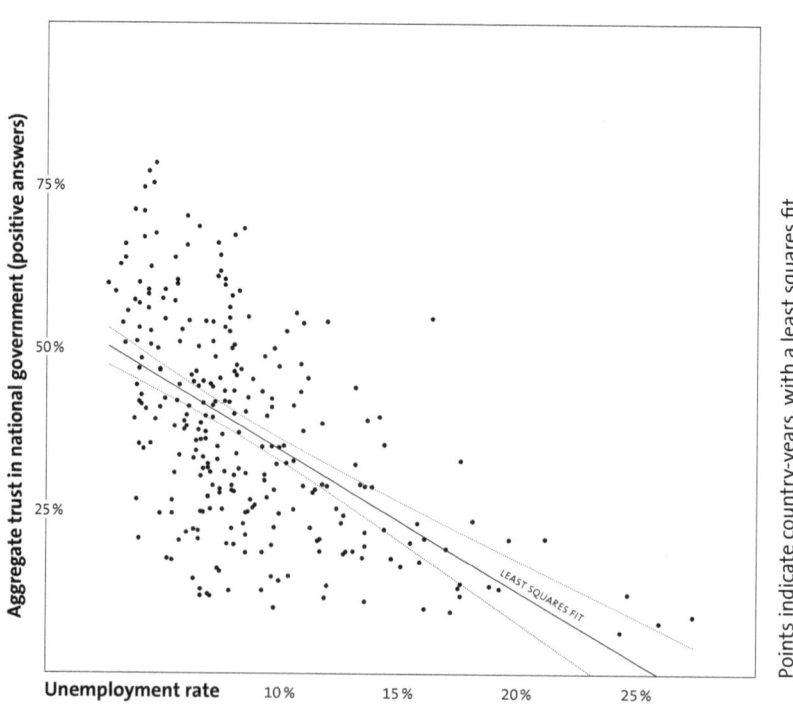

*Figure 5.16* The association between unemployment rates and trust in national governments (2004–2013)

as blame for economic failures can be associated with declining trust in the EU, which is not the case in less economically integrated countries.

Furthermore, the indicators can be used to attempt to rule out alternative explanations. For instance, it may be the case that this pattern is not unique to trust in the EU but also holds true for trust in national governments. This would offer less of an indicator of a problem for governance in the EU and would illustrate more so a general trend in these countries during these points in time.

Figure 5.18 thus conducts the same indicator setup, but looks instead at the relationship between unemployment and trust in national governments. In contrast to Figure 5.17, we see that higher unemployment is significantly associated with declining trust in national governments in almost all categories. This suggests that declining trust in the EU within the five eurozone debt crisis countries, i.e. Greece, Ireland, Italy, Portugal, and Spain, is not simply a general trend also found elsewhere in the EU. Rather, the response and context of the crisis have led to a significant decline in legitimacy that is more pronounced in the five eurozone countries with the highest unemployment rates.

# Conclusion

Interesting stories related to convergence in the EU before and during the current financial crisis have emerged through our indicators. In terms of economic indicators, we can see a number of noteworthy trends. In the years before the financial crisis, a strong trend towards convergence in both unemployment rates and bond yields within the EU was evident. Yet once the crisis hit, this progress was undone, and the subsequent divergence in terms of these indicators reached levels previously unseen in the time period studied. Further inspection revealed the existence of two apparent convergence clubs: eurozone members and non-eurozone members. Whilst eurozone members had converged to a greater extent than non-eurozone members before the crisis, the divergence trend set in motion after the onset of the crisis was significant. In contrast, non-eurozone members did not see such a large divergence after the crisis began and in fact exhibited less variation in unemployment and bond yields during the crisis. Examining time series plots of outcomes within the eurozone members found that the increased variation reflected the particularly bad economic outcomes of the five eurozone countries seemingly hardest hit by the crisis, another possible convergence club to be investigated.

The indicators also shed some light on trends in the EU with regards to public opinion. Here the trend was somewhat similar, yet not identical, to that of economic outcomes. Unlike the economic outcomes studied, there

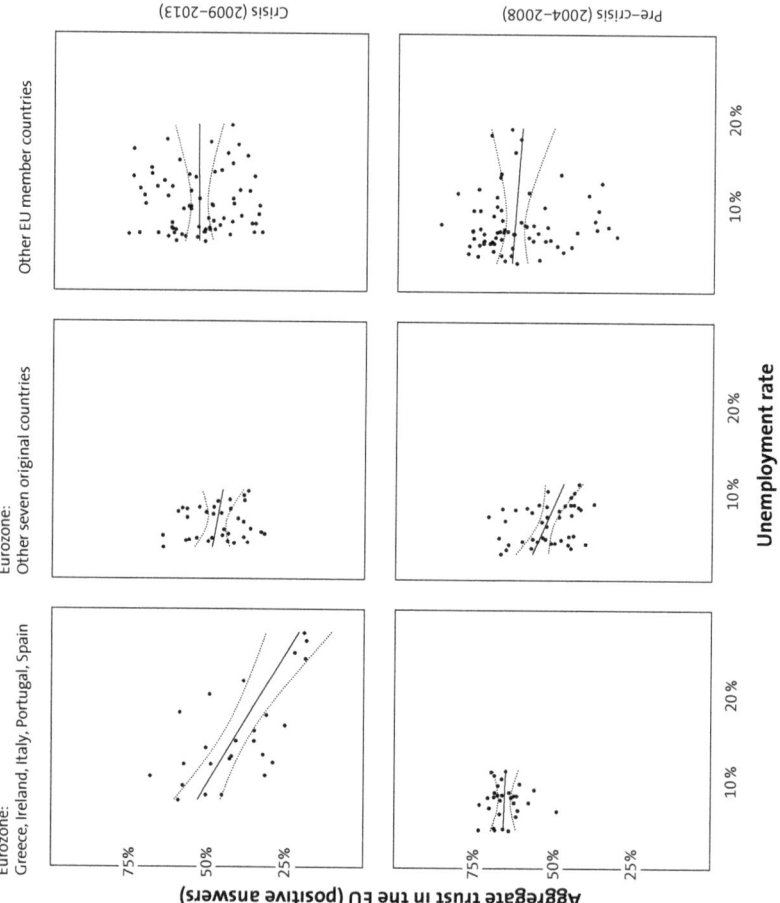

*Figure 5.17* Unemployment rates and trust in the EU, by country grouping, pre-crisis (2004–2008) vs. crisis (2009–2013)

Points indicate country-years, with a least squares fit

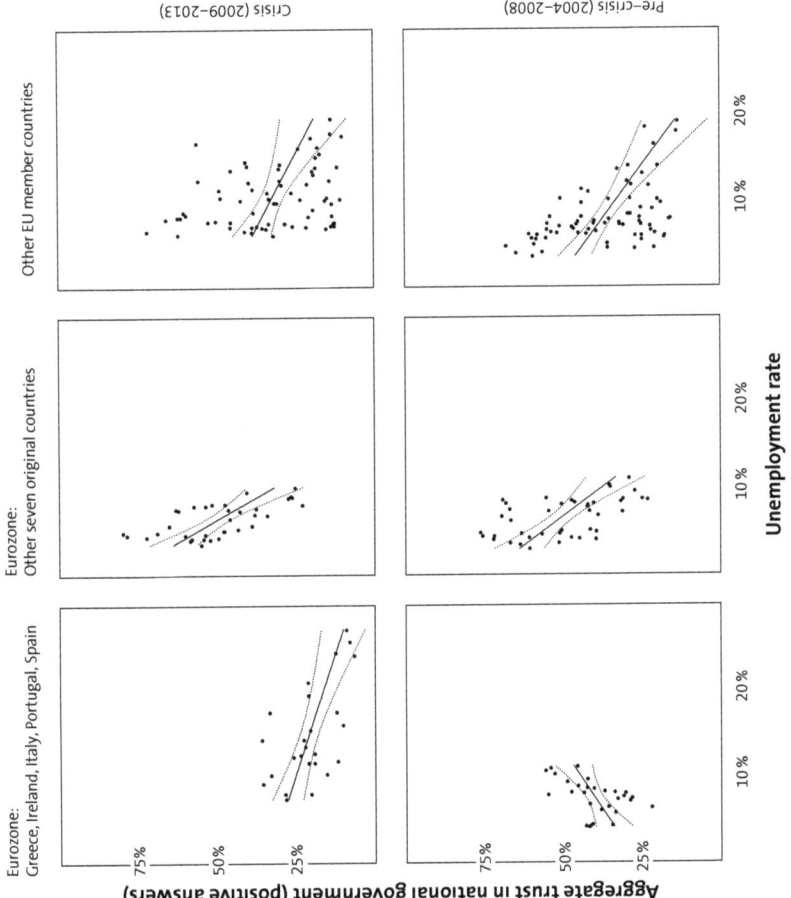

*Figure 5.18* Unemployment rates and trust in national governments, by country grouping, pre-crisis (2004–2008) vs. crisis (2009–2013)

Points indicate country-years, with a least squares fit

GOVERNANCE INDICATORS

was very little change in public opinion patterns within the EU as a whole either before or after the onset of the crisis. Yet a closer inspection of the two convergence clubs–eurozone and non-eurozone members–found that the crisis had set off a pattern of divergence within eurozone countries. With the use of time series plots for the 12 original eurozone members, we found that this pattern was driven by the collapse in trust of the European Parliament within Greece, Ireland, Italy, Portugal, and Spain since the beginning of the crisis. Notably, these countries were amongst those with the highest levels of trust in the European Parliament at the beginning of the 2000s.

Finally, we explored the association between macroeconomic outcomes and public opinion within EU countries. Not surprisingly, we find that unemployment levels and trust in the EU as well as national governments are strongly negatively associated: When unemployment is high, trust is low and vice versa. By pursuing the disaggregation strategy outlined previously–breaking up the associations into the previously identified convergence clubs, as well as the time periods before and after the start of the crisis–we located some notable patterns. In particular, we find that a negative association between unemployment and trust in the EU only exists during the crisis in the context of the five eurozone debt crisis countries. Whilst this may be symptomatic of a general decline in trust as a result of the crisis in those countries, inspecting trust in national governments does not find the same association. Rather, a negative association between unemployment and trust in national governments is not unique to those five countries or to the crisis period. This suggests that, in the five eurozone debt crisis countries in particular, accountability for poor economic outcomes is being transferred to the supranational level of the EU and demonstrates the potential for problems of EU legitimacy in cases of unfavourable domestic economic conditions.

> *In the eurozone debt crisis countries, accountability for poor economic outcomes is transferred to the supranational level, demonstrating the potential for problems of EU legitimacy.*

Our indicators are therefore a useful tool for understanding some of the governance challenges currently faced within the EU. Through the use of time series, we can attempt to identify trends that may worsen or improve these challenges. Whilst some of the findings may not be surprising, the reproduction of previously identified phenomena lends credence to future use of the indicators for identifying issues relating to convergence within the EU that may pose further problems down the road to be tackled with governance measures.

Ultimately, this chapter contains only a small proportion of the trends and associations that can be explored with our indicator set. Further exploration on the Report's website (www.governancereport.org) will allow users to find patterns and convergence clubs that may warrant attention from a governance perspective. In doing so, we hope to provide an important set of tools that can increase understanding of both the past and the future of the EU.

## Endnotes

1. For example, in the study of what constitutes an optimum currency area, the homogeneity (i.e. convergence) of business cycles and labour mobility is important to ensure a successful shared currency (Mundell 1961; Tavlas 1993; Bayoumi and Eichengreen 1994; Frankel and Rose 1998). In addition, divergences in unemployment rates and bond yields, as discussed later, can be indicative of failure to form an optimum currency area.

2. More formally, standard deviation is calculated as $\sqrt{\frac{1}{n-1}\sum_{i=1}^{n}(x_i - \bar{x})^2}$, where $x_i$ is a given country's outcome, $\bar{x}$ is the mean outcome across all countries, and $n$ is the number of observations countries). This can be interpreted as the 'average' deviation from the mean. We also calculate the standard error of the standard deviation as a measure of uncertainty. To do so we use the approximation $\frac{1}{\sqrt{2(n-1)}}\hat{\sigma}$, where $\hat{\sigma}$ is our estimated standard deviation.

3. There exist more complicated statistical techniques for uncovering convergence; however, the focus of these approaches is the *causes* of convergence. As our indicators are a descriptive tool to understand whether convergence has increased or decreased, the sigma approach is sufficient.

4. The 12 countries that joined the euro during the 1999–2001 period are Austria, Belgium, Finland, France, Germany, Ireland, Italy, Luxembourg, the Netherlands, Portugal, Spain, and Greece. Defining the 'original eurozone countries' this way ensures that each country operated under the euro for a significant amount of time prior to the crisis, as opposed to including countries that had joined just before (e.g. Cyprus) or during (e.g. Estonia) the crisis. Other possible convergence club definitions can be found on the Report website (www.governancereport.org).

5. A detailed list of macroeconomic indicators included in our 2015 dashboard can be found at www.governancereport.org/home/governance-indicators. Data from Eurostat Ameco (European Commission 2014).

6. It should be noted that this research (e.g. de Haan 2010) finds that inflation did converge, albeit weakly, in the run up to the adoption of the euro and until the onset of the crisis. This does not however preclude the existence of problems related to differentials between members, even if these differences were smaller than previously.

7. Despite the availability of additional historical data on these two variables, we begin at the year 2000 due to missing data and concerns about comparability of trends. In the case of bond yields, for example, we only have data for 15 countries in the year 1995, compared to 20 countries in 2000 and finally 26 countries in 2006. As the missing data for countries in 1995 is likely due to systematic reasons, we probably would see artificial changes in the convergence estimate if we began at a point with such a small number of observations. Whilst we would ideally start examining bond yields from 2006 onwards, this would not allow us to examine trends for a substantial enough period of time before the occurrence of the eurozone crisis. Therefore, as a trade-off, we compute our measures from the year 2000 onwards.

8. According to Eurostat, long term government bond yields are calculated as monthly averages (non-seasonally adjusted data). They refer to central government bond yields on the secondary market, gross of tax, with a residual maturity of around 10 years. The bond or the bonds of the basket have to be replaced regularly to avoid any maturity drift. This definition is used in the convergence

criteria of the economic and monetary union (EMU) for long-term interest rates, as required under Article 121 of the Treaty of Amsterdam and the Protocol on the convergence criteria.

9   Unlike the data used for EU countries, this data comes from the World Development Indicators (The World Bank). Comparable data for bond yields was unavailable for a large enough sample of non-EU countries.
10  These are also available on the Report website (www.governancereport.org).
11  The estimates of convergence for these aspects start in 2004 due to issues of data availability.

# VI. Outlook
## Where Do the EU and the EMU Go From Here?

MARK DAWSON, HENRIK ENDERLEIN, *and* CHRISTIAN JOERGES

We started this edition of *The Governance Report* with the question: Is the euro crisis over? Our initial answer was 'probably not', but at the time of writing, we can clearly say the crisis is far from finished. This is not only due to short-term challenges, such as the Greek elections that took place in January 2015, but also, and more importantly, due to the long list of open political, legal, and economic questions on the functioning and fundamental structure of the economic and monetary union (EMU).

The euro crisis, the steps taken to manage it, and the resulting transformations have triggered a necessary process of reconsidering economic governance in the European Union (EU). With *The Governance Report 2015*, we contribute to this process by taking an interdisciplinary approach. Undoubtedly, the eurozone crisis has challenged all academic disciplines. From quite different angles, the chapters in this Report have taken stock of the current situation by tracing both the origins of the problems brought to light by the crisis as well as the dilemmas that must be recognised and addressed in order to move ahead. The goal of this combined effort has never been to develop some kind of 'super-strategy' on how to get things right but rather to shed light on the challenges ahead and on the options we have for continuing the process.

> The euro crisis, the steps taken to manage it, and the resulting transformations have triggered a necessary process of reconsidering economic governance in the EU.

### Where We Are Now

At the time of writing, the eurozone economy looks very fragile. Growth rates in most eurozone member states are at historical lows or even negative. Unemployment remains high. There still is a real risk of deflation. In normal times, the economic policy-making toolkit would allow policy-makers to counter such negative trends with a mix of demand-side measures, including lower interest rates and fiscal stimuli, and supply-side measures, such as reforms and structural improvements to the economy. But times are still not normal. Interest rates are already at zero. Debt levels in many countries are so high that further stimuli would threaten their repayment capacity. While most countries in difficulties took great strides to implement structural reforms in their economies, the political backlash against such reforms is now considerable. Eurosceptic and Europhobic parties are on the rise. Crisis and reform fatigue are a key feature of domestic politics in the eurozone today.

Also, as this Report has shown, the EMU itself remains incomplete. There are good reasons to believe that the economic and monetary union is not viable in its current form in the long run, although a number of quick fixes have been implemented during the crisis. At a time of high political contestation of the European project, it seems difficult to push forward an agenda for reform of the EMU. Calls for enhanced EU legitimacy are getting louder, and the economic crisis has brought institutional change. But institutional change has not yet been followed by further political integration.

In this sense, while it is tempting to see the changes brought on by the euro crisis within existing understandings of EU integration, the crisis requires a reconsideration of how we view the EU's basic decision-making structures. Most debate has depicted the crisis as either creating greater technocratic supranational steering, particularly of national budgetary decisions, or leading down the opposite path. Within the latter view, the central hegemonic position of the German Chancellor and the rise of institutions such as the European Council and Eurogroup illustrate a growing reassertion of national control over the EU project.

In reality, the crisis has led us down both paths. As Chapter 3 of this Report has argued, the crisis has witnessed the generalisation of a novel coordinative method of EU governance that combines heightened EU supervision of how member states implement EU policies with greater intergovernmental steering of key substantive decisions. In order to combine the paradoxical need for greater common EU fiscal discipline with the desire to retain ultimate political and fiscal control at the member state level, national leaders have transformed the way in which EU decision-making in the fiscal field operates.

In doing so, however, those same leaders have also transformed the available means by which EU decision-makers can be held accountable. At a legal level, the reliance under EU economic governance on discretionary fiscal standards and the increasing use of international law agreements among member states has made it more difficult for citizens to exercise their rights of individual judicial review. At a political level, the rise of executive institutions in the fiscal field, such as the Eurogroup or European Central Bank (ECB), has correlated with the tendency to marginalise parliamentary institutions, with the European Parliament (EP) in particular gaining limited decision-making power in the fiscal field. If the crisis has established new EU authority, it has not (yet) established the mechanisms of control needed to render EU economic decision-making legally and politically accountable.

The compromise about the institutionalisation of EMU was in conceptual terms a compromise between Germany's ordo-liberal economic stability philosophy and the French prioritisation of political guidance. That compromise was not only conceptually incoherent in the realm of monetary policy. It also failed to provide for effective instruments for solving conflict constellations that were bound to arise from the tensions between the powers of the member states in fiscal and economic policy on the one hand and the exclusive competence of the Union in monetary policy on the other. These powers were assigned to different levels of governance, but the Treaties remained silent as to the definition of monetary policy. Supremacy could not be claimed with respect to fiscal and monetary policy. The interdependence between these policy fields was left to soft mechanisms of coordination and an ongoing search for compromises and political bargaining.

The ensuing conflict constellation was paradoxical. The deepening of integration in the sphere of monetary policy generated disintegrative effects. Contrary to expectations, the Europeanisation of monetary policy did not promote socioeconomic convergence. While the common currency facilitated access to financial markets, it did not affect the institutional infrastructure of national economies and the social norms prevailing in European societies. The resulting tensions were kept latent only provisionally: When the financial crisis hit Europe, it became readily apparent that the imperfections of economic integration threatened the governability of the EU.

The institutionalisation of EMU was not guided by the principle of precaution. A failure or malfunction was simply not foreseen. The order of competences and the regulatory instruments in place did not suffice to organise responses in an emergency situation. It is hence unsurprising that the EU's crisis management replaced the Community method with a resort to international agreements and unconventional rescue mechanisms. The safeguarding of the stability of the euro area as a whole became henceforward the highest priority.

This defence of the common currency came at a price, however. Having to take the diversity of national economies and societies into account, the EU's crisis management operated in a highly discretionary fashion and thereby disregarded the European commitment to the rule of law. An evaluation of the responses to crisis in terms of democratic legitimacy seems even more disquieting. The interdependencies between the member state economies required interventions that were accommodated with deliberative processes in the democratically legitimated institutions only under harsh constraints. Within the eurozone, the only means available to struggling member states to strengthen their competitiveness has been 'internal devaluation', i.e., the turn to austerity politics.

Hence, the EU's crisis management has affected the two main pillars of legitimate rule in constitutional democracies, namely the stability of the economic system and the protection of social welfare. As a consequence, the European project is no longer identified with economic welfare and social progress. Indeed, the tensions between economic integration and democratic legitimacy have intensified. As Chapter 5 on governance indicators documents in detail, these tensions are by no means simply theoretical conjectures; they are very real tendencies. Economic outcomes such as unemployment resonate with social acceptance of and trust in the EU to such a degree that further integration within the EU might lead to further problems of legitimacy in cases where domestic economic conditions are not favourable.

## Where We Go from Here

Exploratory governance–introduced in the first chapter of this Report as an approach for thinking about highly salient, highly contestable, and highly risky policy choices under extreme uncertainty–emphasises that there comes a time when decision-makers must choose between uncertain paths in terms of future policy-making. Those paths are generally either: to discontinue the newly adopted governance structures and return to the old; to continue with the new structures; or to amend the new structures. The euro crisis has made it clear that the EMU is now at the point where decisions have to be taken about which of those paths is worth following.

*The EMU is now at the point where decisions have to be taken about which path is worth following.*

The first option–returning to old structures–is not desirable. Newly introduced instruments have sought to neutralise errors in the foundation of the economic governance framework, some with admittedly more success than others. Abandoning this path would mean returning to an inherently unsound regime.

Continuing under current arrangements–the second option–also appears to be untenable. The existing economic governance regime is the result of decision-making under the extreme pressure of the crisis. Its primary goal has been to stabilise the eurozone and maintain the EMU at all costs. However, the system now in place leaves significant accountability gaps and lacks the original regime's legitimacy base.

Therefore, the third option–correcting the current path, probably through another round of exploratory governance–seems to be the most likely way forward. Different disciplines offer different ideas. As we highlight in our respective chapters, we offer no economic, political, or legal blueprint plan or grand interdisciplinary strategy, but rather considerations that should be part of the discussions about the future of economic governance in the EU.

## Economic governance

As Chapter 2 in this Report has argued, in the first 15 years of its existence, the eurozone has been characterised by large structural heterogeneities between countries and the absences of the so-called 'optimum currency area criteria' and functional equivalents of those criteria, such as a common budget, common taxes, automatic cyclical stabilisers, and high labour mobility.

### Recommendation 1: Enhance structural convergence.

Structural convergence needs to be built between countries so as to allow for better functioning of the single currency, in particular due to an improved monetary policy transmission mechanism and an enhanced price transmission (real exchange rate effect).

For the same reasons, the single market should be completed in order to end a situation in which economic developments are to a very large extent shaped by domestic, and not eurozone, factors. Reforming the single market therefore offers a high potential for growth and is necessary in order to mitigate the pro-cyclical effects of the ECB's single monetary policy that were among the causes of the euro crisis. Freer movement of goods and services in the eurozone could lead to a strengthening of the real exchange rate channel, which in turn would work against the build-up of cyclical divergences between eurozone countries. The service sector is an especially promising target: It accounts for 70 per cent of the EU's GDP, but only 20 per cent of services are traded cross-border.

Also, structural reforms in domestic economies must continue to allow for an increase of potential growth and high employment rates. Even if the assessment on overall reform needs might be quite straightforward, the exact content and degree of structural reforms for reaching convergence and enhancing growth is the subject of considerable debate.

### Recommendation 2: Enhance cyclical convergence.

The question of a fiscal stabilisation mechanism that would act towards synchronising business cycles in the eurozone should also be put on the agenda. As long as cyclical heterogeneities are high and labour mobility is low, there should be a stabilising instrument. This proposal was already featured in the original Delors Report (Delors 1989) and taken up again in the Four Presidents' Report of 2012 (van Rompuy et al. 2012). Several proposals are still on the table and range from partial European unemployment insurance via reinsurance at the EU level to output gap-based cyclical shock insurance that would not even require a budget. Many of these proposals address similar issues. It is important to embrace them.

**Recommendation 3: Rethink the relationship between solidarity and conditionality.**

Most political difficulties in the euro crisis have arisen as a consequence of strong disagreements between member states on how to solve the trade-off between solidarity and conditionality. Granting support to countries in financial distress in forms of liquidity or fiscal support can become an unavoidable feature of a monetary union that doesn't allow exit. To illustrate: Were Greek banks to not receive 'emergency liquidity assistance' from the ECB, then the Greek banking system would be likely to collapse and trigger Greece's forced exit from the eurozone. As a consequence, the crisis has seen an array of rescue measures aimed at ensuring that there was no threat of a member state exit. At the same time, those measures were implemented as quid pro quos, asking recipient countries to undertake reforms, cut spending, or sell public assets. Today, both the creditor and debtor sides question those practices. On one side there is fear of a 'transfer union'. On the other side there is fear of an erosion of democracy. Europe thus needs a well-considered scheme that ensures a lender of last resort while avoiding the creation of incentives for irresponsible fiscal policy. One way to solve the matter could be a system of 'federalism by exception' (Delors and Enderlein 2012) based on the idea that sovereignty in a monetary union ends when solvency ends. While the nucleus of such a scheme has already been implemented with the Troika programmes (cf. Chapter 3), further work is needed to make the balance between solidarity and conditionality more transparent, predictable, and legitimate.

## Institutional dilemmas

Chapter 3 of this report has argued that institutional responses to the crisis must pay attention not only to the functional needs of the EMU but also to the serious accountability gaps forged by the EU's response to the crisis. A pressing challenge for the European Union now is to seek a structure for legal and political accountability in EU economic governance that will allow citizens to contest and challenge the decisions shaping their lives.

**Recommendation 4: Close the political accountability gap at the supranational and national levels.**

At both levels such a structure would involve a different kind of parliamentary involvement in economic decision-making. At the EU level, the significant distributive impact of EU economic decisions suggests that the 'communitarisation' of fiscal decision-making should be an urgent priority. This requires the European Parliament to engage in an 'economic dialogue' with the other EU institutions and carry a decision-making veto over key instruments of fiscal governance, such as economic partnerships and conditionality programmes between the EU and its member states. Meanwhile, at the national level, the EP should see cooperation between national parliaments not as a threat to its prerogatives but rather, national parliaments as crucial allies in holding executive decision-makers at the national and EU levels to account. A strong interparliamentary conference on economic governance, held on dates coordinated with major EU-level decision points, could go some way towards rebalancing how power under EU economic governance is exercised.

**Recommendation 5: The EU and national courts should open up rather than close down pathways for individuals to contest and challenge economic decision-making.**

At both the national and supranational levels, the European courts should not shy away from examining links between economic governance and other parts of EU law, including the compatibility of economic measures with EU fundamental rights. In this regard, the European courts can play a crucial role in mediating increasingly likely substantive and procedural conflicts between eurozone and non-eurozone states. At the member state level, national courts in an increasingly integrated EU carry a responsibility not only to uphold their own domestic constitutional frameworks but also to take into account the impact of their rulings on the constitutional principles and rights of other member states. Regular interactions between these courts and the European Court of Justice (ECJ), as well as judicial networks between national constitutional courts, are a crucial tool for ensuring that national courts seek more dialogue both with EU courts and one another.

## Regaining legitimacy

As noted earlier, there are obvious tensions between economic integration and democratic legitimacy. These tensions have accompanied the integration project from early on and have gradually intensified with its deepening. Though they have often been camouflaged, such complacency would by now be counterproductive. Even if we can methodologically and theoretically distinguish between functional necessities, institutional developments, and the transformation of governance practices, we cannot insulate them from normative concerns and political contestation. We even have to concede that the search for what is functionally required has to operate under high uncertainty and has hence to remain exploratory. Further, we have to realise that the effectiveness of new modes of economic governance and intense coordination remains dependent upon conditions and circumstances which cannot be created or imposed by legal fiat.

**Recommendation 6: Reject normalisation of crisis governance.**

With respect to the legitimacy *problématique* Chapter 4 has juxtaposed the alternatives of 'normalisation', i.e. readiness to accept the new realities of crisis governance as circumstances we have to adapt to, and 'contestation', i.e., the search for a renewed constitutional condition which 'deserves recognition'. All of our inquiries point to what the indicators presented in Chapter 5 signal: EU governance is inevitably exposed to ever more intense claims and controversies. On this basis it is safe to conclude that we should take the integration project's exposure to political contestation as a given and focus instead on the modes of contestation and the potential to regain legitimacy. This path is by no means without risks of its own. The outcome of contestation over economic and social conditions is by its very nature unpredictable. What is conceivable, however, is that such debates can be channelled so as to ensure their deliberative quality.

The suggestions developed in Chapter 3 and above point precisely in that direction. In seeking to strengthen accountability towards EU citizens, the recommendations rely on the involvement of democratically legitimated actors and plead for the opening of new fora for such debate. They envisage a re-parliamentarisation of EU politics not only at the EU level but also through interparliamentary cooperation. The suggestions on the potential role of national constitutional courts follow the same pattern. No single European court, the CJEU included, can claim to be the sole guardian of European constitutionalism. These suggestions are not merely utopian. They build upon well-documented processes, in particular parliamentary initiatives. Within the European judiciary, steps towards an interactive adjudication can be observed even between the seemingly obstinate German Constitutional Court and the CJEU.

Chapter 2 opens a third avenue with the plea for a new understanding of the relationship between solidarity and conditionality. This suggestion is again not merely a normative claim but has a factual background. The organisers of structural reforms have to avoid the pretence of knowledge that is simply unavailable and remain aware of the dependence of implementation processes on local knowledge and cooperation. 'Conditionality' may profit normatively and factually through its reconceptualisation as cooperative problem-solving.

**Recommendation 7: Embrace contestation as a chance for constructive innovation and allow for more diversity.**

Through the involvement of new actors and the strengthening of cooperative, rather than hierarchical, structures, the kind of openings advocated here may foster a return to a greater variety of institutional configurations and practices. This need not be perceived as a price we have to pay for the unruliness of the EU. Contestation has innovative potentials and can reveal new insights and perspectives. More institutional diversity can be economically beneficial rather than detrimental.

## Exploratory Governance (Continues)

Each of the aspects that we have examined–the functioning of the EMU, institutional transformation and accountability gaps, and the legitimacy *problématique*–has a significant bearing on the viability of the others. The interconnectedness of the challenges currently faced by the European Union is a large part of what makes choosing the right political and institutional approach so difficult.

Exploratory governance will thus have to continue. Even if there were an agreement on the economic challenges and ways to fix them–and there is no such agreement just yet–the ensuing political and legal challenges would still be considerable. The EMU cannot function optimally or sustainably if its economic governance structures are not accountable and have little legitimacy, and an economic and monetary union that does not function will not be able to gain, much less retain, legitimacy. Indeed, depending on the answers to the all of the questions above, there are different legal and political requirements. It is often unclear which proposals would require treaty change and, if treaty changes were needed, which variants in the large array of possible forms of treaty change and treaty change procedures. It is also often unclear how new elements could be anchored in appropriate democratic control mechanisms in order to ensure their legitimacy. The question of the possible participation of national parliaments is often raised in that respect.

*Recognising that the economic and monetary union will continue to be a work in progress could be a first step towards improving the policy debate.*

We suggest that political and legal questions must be considered in light of the functional discussion on the completion of the EMU. It also would be politically naïve to believe that a functional debate could be started without taking into account the legal and political constraints. Striking the right balance in that trade-off situation is a considerable challenge in itself.

*The Governance Report 2015* has tried to sketch out the method of exploratory governance as a way to deal with this trade-off and, more generally, with situations of policy-making complexity, characterised by many 'known unknowns' but even more 'unknown unknowns'. In such contexts, it can make more sense to try to find the right working method rather than to try to find the answers to every open question. There will never be such a thing as a full-fledged blueprint for the completion of the EMU. However, recognising that the economic and monetary union will continue to be a work in progress could be a first step towards improving the policy debate. Exploratory governance will always be characterised by uncertainty and a lack of orientation in unchartered territory, but this shouldn't stop policy-makers from trying to make progress.

# Appendix
# The Main Treaties of the European Union

## Treaties of Rome: European Economic Community and European Atomic Energy Community

In 1957, the Treaty establishing the European Economic Community (EEC) and the Treaty establishing the European Atomic Energy Community (Euroatom) were signed by France, Germany, Italy, Belgium, Luxemburg, and the Netherlands. It was the EEC treaty that created a common market, a customs union, and common policies aimed at promoting economic development, expansion, stability, a higher standard of living, and closer relations among its members. The treaty introduced the notion of 'an ever closer union among the peoples of Europe', thereby laying the foundation for the integration processes that followed.

At the centre of the common market stood the four freedoms of free movement of persons, services, goods, and capital. Additionally, common policies in the areas of agriculture, trade, and transport were developed. This initial integration was supported through the establishment of institutions and a decision-making mechanism. A key role in the decision-making process–the drafting of proposals–was given to the Commission, an independent body appointed by common agreement among the member states. The Council of Ministers–known today as the Council of the European Union or simply, the Council–represented the member states' governments and decided on drafts from the Commission. A Parliamentary Assembly was also part of the institutional set-up of the EEC, although its members were delegates from national parliaments and had merely observer and advisory roles.

When the Treaty of Lisbon entered into force in December 2009, the European Community (the name used for the EEC after 1993) ceased to exist, and the treaty establishing the EEC was renamed the Treaty on the Functioning of the European Union (TFEU).

# Single European Act (SEA)

The Single European Act (SEA) of 1986 represented an important step towards further integration. In an amendment to the Treaty establishing the European Economic Community (EEC), the SEA aimed to complete the internal market by establishing a single market with not only a customs union and a common economic area, but also common policies in areas beyond trade. New competences included social and environment policy, research, and technical development, as well as calls for a common European foreign policy and consultations among member states on common security issues.

A major revision in the EEC's decision-making mechanism was the move from unanimity to qualified majority voting in the Council of Ministers. In addition, the formalised meeting of heads of state and government was institutionalised as an official body in the EEC, albeit without any role in the decision-making process.

Having gained more weight through direct election in 1979, the European Parliament (EP) was further strengthened with the SEA, and its decision-making mechanism was extended to include a cooperation and assent procedure: In a limited number of areas (e.g. enlargement of the EU), the Parliament must concur with the Council's proposal. The cooperation procedure consists of two readings, during which the Parliament may propose changes and reject the Council's position.

# Maastricht Treaty or Treaty on European Union (TEU)

The Maastricht Treaty, which entered into force in 1993, took integration to a new level by bringing the existing structures under the umbrella of the newly created European Union. It consisted of three pillars: the original 'communities' (i.e. European Economic Community (EEC, later renamed European Community), European Coal and Steel Community (ECSC), and European Atomic Energy Community (Euroatom)); the Common Foreign and Security Policy (CFSP) as the second pillar, with strong roles for the member states; and the area of justice and home affairs as the third pillar, again dominated by the member states.

Significantly, the signatories to the treaty agreed to institutionalise the economic and monetary union (EMU), which included not only stronger coordination of economic and monetary policies, but also the creation of a single common currency. Authority over monetary policy was transferred to the newly created European System of Central Banks (ESCB).

For the European Parliament (EP), the treaty meant more influence. The cooperation and assent procedure was extended to other areas, and the codecision procedure was introduced: In up to three readings, the Council and the Parliament are required to agree on a proposal for a new act. Additionally, the Parliament became part of the Commission confirmation process. The treaty broadened EU involvement to additional policy areas including consumer protection for which competence is shared and industrial policy and culture for which the EU plays a supporting role (see Box 3.2).

Clearly showing the progress of European integration, the treaty also institutionalised European citizenship, which grants citizens of EU member states the rights to travel and reside in every EU country, as well as to vote and run in municipal elections in a country of residence.

## Treaty of Amsterdam

Signed in 1997, the Treaty of Amsterdam aimed to simplify existing structures in order to accommodate the growing number of EU member states.

For example, the decision-making mechanism in the Common Foreign and Security Policy (CFSP) shifted from unanimity to qualified majority voting, with a few exceptions still requiring unanimity. The position of a High Representative for the CFSP was established, thereby assigning more weight to foreign and security policy at the EU level.

The European Parliament (EP) also gained additional importance in terms of decision-making procedures. The codecision procedure by which the Council and Parliament were required to agree was extended to cover most legislative acts, whilst the procedure itself was reduced from three to two readings: If the Council and Parliament are not able to find a compromise during those stages, the proposal is rejected. In addition, the treaty limited the number of seats in the Parliament.

Many institutional protocols contained within the Amsterdam Treaty were designed to prepare the Union for enlargement: for example, that the Commission would include one representative from each member state, and that in the case of the Council, a decision-making reform at the time of the next enlargement would address potential overrepresentation of small and medium-sized countries.

The question of democratic legitimacy was addressed by extending the jurisdiction of the Court of Justice to include the treaty's fundamental rights, asylum and migration issues, and police and judicial cooperation. The treaty also introduced the possibility of closer cooperation among member states in the areas of the Treaty of Rome (e.g. tax, economic, and employment policy) and in police and judicial matters. This closer cooperation must meet several conditions such as being in accordance with the Treaty of Rome, concerning the majority of member states, and allowing all member states to participate at any time.

## Treaty of Nice

Signed by the then-15 member states in 2001 and entering into force in 2003, the Treaty of Nice aimed to prepare the EU for enlargement. As stipulated in the Treaty of Amsterdam, the Council's voting mechanism needed to be revised before the accession of new member states. As a result, the Treaty of Nice adjusted the number of votes by population size and redefined the qualified majority in the Council, as well as introduced a second majority rule: the demographic clause. Council members can request to ensure not only a qualified majority of votes but also that this majority represents at least 62 per cent of the EU's population.

The treaty fixed the number of Commissioners at one per member state, with states appointing Commission members by a qualified majority instead of unanimity, and the entire college of Commissioners then being approved by the European Parliament (EP). The same procedure applies to the President of the Commission. After being nominated by the European Council, i.e. the heads of state and government, with a qualified majority, the Parliament must approve the candidate. The President was also equipped with more power, including laying down the principles of the Commission's work and allocating responsibilities.

In view of enlargement, the treaty restructured the EU's judicial system to ensure efficiency. The composition of the Court of First Instance (CFI) and the Court of Justice was determined as one judge per member state in each court, and to accommodate the growing number of cases, the jurisdiction of the Court of First Instance was extended.

## Treaty of Lisbon

The Treaty of Lisbon followed the unsuccessful attempt to reform the European Union through the establishment of a Constitution for Europe, which had failed to be ratified in several member states. Signed in 2007 and entered into force in 2009, the Treaty of Lisbon amended existing treaties to encompass the needs of a Union with then-27 member states.

Most importantly, the treaty abolished the pillar structure set up by the Maastricht Treaty (or Treaty on European Union, TEU) in 1993. The three 'communities' ceased to exist and were replaced by a single legal entity, the European Union.

In an effort to enhance democratic legitimacy, the European Parliament (EP) was given an even greater role in the decision-making process. The codecision procedure was renamed an 'ordinary legislative procedure' and applied to more policy areas, including agriculture and immigration. The EP's control over the budget became equal with the Council, and the Parliament gained greater influence on the Commission by directly electing the Commission's President and confirming the Commission itself. The introduction of the citizen's initiative–the possibility of bringing forward a proposal to the Commission by collecting at least one million signatures from several member states–aimed at bringing citizens into the decision-making process.

In the institutional setup of the EU, the European Council encompassing the heads of state and government was formally recognised as a body of the EU. The introduction of a permanent President of the European Council was a significant change from a six-month presidency rotating amongst member states. The Council (of Ministers) maintained its role in the legislative procedure, although the internal decision-making procedure was revised, abolishing the system of vote weighting. With the Lisbon Treaty, 55 per cent of member states representing at least 65 per cent of the EU population is necessary to decide on a proposal from the Commission. The Commission was also enhanced with the new position of the High Representative of the Union for Foreign Affairs and Security Policy.

For further information see:
http://europa.eu/eu-law/decision-making/treaties/index_en.htm
(as of February 2015)

# References

Abelshauser, W. (2014). Europa in Vielfalt einigen. Eine Denkschrift. Bielefeld: Universität Bielefeld.

Abelshauser, W. (2013). 'E pluribus unum? Eine alternative Strategie für Europa', *Zeitschrift für Staats- und Europawissenschaften*, 11(4): 466–83.

Abelshauser, W. (2004). *Deutsche Wirtschaftsgeschichte seit 1945*. Munich: Beck.

Abelshauser, W., Gilgen, D., and Leutzsch, A. (eds) (2012). *Kulturen der Weltwirtschaft*. Göttingen: Vandenhoeck & Ruprecht.

Armstrong, K. (2013). 'The New Governance of EU Fiscal Discipline', *European Law Review*, 38(5): 601–17.

Azoulai, L. (2013). 'The European Court of Justice and the Duty to Respect Sensitive National Interests', in M. Dawson, B. de Witte, and E. Muir (eds), *Judicial Activism at the European Court of Justice: Causes, Responses and Solutions*. Cheltenham: Edward Elgar, 167–87.

Bach, M. (forthcoming). 'Paradoxical Europe: The Euro Crisis and its (own Internal) Dynamics', in M. Dawson, H. Enderlein, and C. Joerges (eds), *The Transformation of the European Union: Challenges of Functionality, Design and Democratic Legitimacy*. Oxford: Oxford University Press.

Bayoumi, T., and Eichengreen, B. (1994). *One Money or Many? Analysing the Prospects for Monetary Unification in Various Parts of the World*. Princeton Studies in International Finance 76. Princeton: Department of Economics, Princeton University.

Bekker, S. (2013). The EU's Stricter Economic Governance: A Step Towards More Binding Coordination of Social Policies?. Discussion Paper SP IV 2013–501. Berlin: WZB (Social Science Research Center Berlin).

Benz, A. (2013). 'An Asymmetric Two-Level Game: Parliaments in the Euro Crisis', in B. Crum, and J. E. Fossum (eds), *Practices of Interparliamentary Coordination in International Politics: The European Union and Beyond*. Colchester: ECPR Press, 125–40.

Bernauer, T., and Achini, C. (2000). 'From "Real" to "Virtual" States?: Integration of the World Economy and its Effects on Government Activity', *European Journal of International Relations*, 6(2): 223–76.

Biedenkopf, K. (2012). *Der Weg zum Euro. Stationen einer verpassten Chance: Ausgewählte Aufzeichnungen*. Berlin: Hertie School of Governance.

BMWi (Bundesministerium für Wirtschaft) (1986). Stellungnahme zum Weissbuch der EG-Kommission über den Binnenmarkt. Gutachten des Wissenschaftlichen Beirats beim Bundesministerium für Wirtschaft. Bonn: BMWi.

Böckenförde, E.-W. (2010). 'Kennt die europäische Not kein Gebot?: Die Webfehler der EU und die Notwendigkeit einer neuen politischen Entscheidung', *Neue Zürcher Zeitung*, 26 June 2010: 22.

Böckenförde, E.-W. (1978). 'Der verdrängte Ausnahmezustand. Zum Handeln der Staatsgewalt in außergewöhnlichen Lagen', *Neue Juristische Wochenschrift*, 31: 1881–90.

Böhm, F. (1989). 'Rule of Law in a Market Economy', in A. T. Peacock, and H. Willgerodt (eds), *Germany's Social Market Economy: Origins and Evolution*. New York: St. Martin's Press, 46–67.

Böll, S. (2011) [website]. *Biedenkopf erklärt die Krise*. Retrieved from http://www.spiegel.de/wirtschaft/euro-crashkurs-biedenkopf-erklaert-die-krise-a-800660.html (accessed 6 Febuary 2015).

Braams, B. (2013). *Koordinierung als Kompetenzkategorie*. Tübingen: Mohr Siebeck.

BVerfGE (Bundesverfassungsgericht) (2014). 2 BvR 1390/12, Judgment of 18 March 2014.

BVerfGE (Bundesverfassungsgericht) (2011). *EFS*, 2 BvR 987/10, 2 BvR 1485/10, 2 BvR 1099/10, Judgment of 7 September 2011.

BVerfGE (Bundesverfassungsgericht) (1998). *Euro*, 2 BvR 1877/97, BVerfGE 97, 350, Judgment of 31 March 1998.

BVerfGE (Bundesverfassungsgericht) (1993). *Maastricht*, 2 BvR 2134/92, 2 BvR 2159/92, BVerfGE 89, 155, Judgment of 12 January 1993.

CEC (Commission of the European Communities) (1985). Completing the Internal Market. White Paper from the Commission to the European Council, COM (58) 310 final. Brussels: CEC.

Chalmers, D. (2013). European Restatements of Sovereignty. LSE Law, Society and Economy Working Papers 10/2013. London: LSE.

Chalmers, D. (2012). 'The European Redistributive State and a European Law of Struggle', *European Law Journal*, 18(5): 667–93.

Chalmers, D., and Chaves, M. (2014). 'EU Law-Making and the State of European Democratic Agency', in O. Cramme, and S. B. Hobolt (eds), *Democratic Politics in a European Union Under Stress*. Oxford: Oxford University Press, 155–179.

Claeys, G., Hallerberg, M., and Tschekassin, O. (2014). European Central Bank Accountability: How the Monetary Dialogue Could Evolve. Bruegel Policy Contribution 2014/04. Brussels: Bruegel.

Clark, W. R., Copelovitch, M., Hallerberg, M., Quaglia, L., and Walter, S. (2013). 'Challenge in Focus: Financial and Fiscal Governance', in Hertie School of Governance (ed), *The Governance Report 2013*. Oxford: Oxford University Press, 59–82.

Cooper, I. (2014). Parliamentary Oversight of the EU After the Crisis. On the Creation of the 'Article 13' Interparliamentary Conference. Working Paper SOG-WP21/2014. Rome: LUISS Guido Carli School of Government.

CJEU (Court of Justice of the European Union) (2015). Opinion of Advocate General Cruz Villalón Delivered on 14 January 2015. Case C-62/14.

CJEU (Court of Justice of the European Union) (2014a). *Bundesdruckerei GmbH v Stadt Dortmund*, C-549/13, Judgment of 18 September 2014.

CJEU (Court of Justice of the European Union) (2014b). Ålands *vindkraft AB v Energimyndigheten*, C-573/12, Judgment of 1 July 2014.

CJEU (Court of Justice of the European Union) (2012). *Thomas Pringle v Government of Ireland*, C-370/12, Judgment of 27 November 2012.

CJEU (Court of Justice of the European Union) (2008). *Dirk Rüffert v Land Niedersachsen*, C-346/06, [2008] ECR I-01989, Judgment of 3 April 2008.

CJEU (Court of Justice of the European Union) (2007a). *Laval un Partneri Ltd v Svenska Byggnadsarbetareförbundet*, C-341/05, [2007] ECR I-11767, Judgment of 18 December 2007.

CJEU (Court of Justice of the European Union) (2007b). *International Transport Workers' Federation and Finnish Seamen's Union v Viking Line ABP and OÜ Viking Line Eesti*, C-438/05, [2007] ECR I-10779, Judgment of 11 December 2007.

CJEU (Court of Justice of the European Union) (2003). *Altmark Trans GmbH and Regierungspräsidium Magdeburg v Nahverkehrsgesellschaft Altmark GmbH*, C-280/00, [2003] ECR I-07747, Judgment of 24 July 2003.

CJEU (Court of Justice of the European Union) (1999a). *Albany*, Case C-67/96, [1999] ECR I-05751, Judgment of 21 September 1999.

CJEU (Court of Justice of the European Union) (1999b). *Drijvende*, C-213/97, [1999] ECR I-06121, Judgment of 21 September 1999.

Crum, B. (2013). 'Saving the Euro at the Cost of Democracy?', *Journal of Common Market Studies*, 51(4): 614–30.

Curtin, D. (2014). 'Challenging Executive Dominance in European Democracy', in C. Joerges, and C. Glinski (eds), *The European Crisis and the Transformation of Transnational Governance: Authoritarian Managerialism Versus Democratic Governance*. Oxford: Hart Publishing, 203–26.

Curtin, D. (2009). *Executive Power of the European Union: Laws, Practices and the Living Constitution*. Oxford: Oxford University Press.

Dawson, M. (2011). *New Governance and the Transformation of European Law: Coordinating EU Social Law and Policy*. Cambridge: Cambridge University Press.

Dawson, M., and de Witte, F. (2013). 'Constitutional Balance in the EU After the Euro Crisis', *The Modern Law Review*, 76(5): 817–44.

Deakin, S. (2014). 'Social Policy, Economic Governance and EMU: Alternatives to Austerity', in N. Bruun, K. Lörcher, and I. Schömann (eds), *The Economic and Financial Crisis and Collective Labour Law in Europe*. Oxford: Hart Publishing, 83–106.

de Grauwe, P. (2011). Governance of a Fragile Eurozone, CEPS Working Documents 346. Brussels: Centre for European Policy Studies.

de Haan, J.(2010). 'Inflation Differentials in the Euro Area: A Survey', in J. de Haan, and H. Berger (eds), *The European Central Bank at Ten*. Berlin: Springer, 11–32.

de Visser, M., and Claes, M. (2013). 'Courts United?: On European Judicial Networks', in A. Vauchez, and B. de Witte (eds), *Lawyering Europe: European Law as a Transnational Social Field*. Oxford: Hart Publishing.

Dehousse, R. (ed) (2011). *The Community Method: Obstinate or Obsolete?* Basingstoke: Palgrave Macmillan.

Dehousse, R., and Weiler, J. H. H. (1990). 'The Legal Dimension', in W. Wallace (ed), *The Dynamics of European Integration*. London: Pinter Publishers for the Royal Institute of International Affairs, 242–60.

Delors, J. (1989). Report on Economic and Monetary Union in the European Community. Brussels: European Council.

Delors, J., and Enderlein, H. (2012). Reform Proposals for the Euro Zone. Paris: Notre Europe - Jacques Delors Institute.

DG ECFIN (Directorate-General for Economic and Financial Affairs) (1990). One Market, One Money: An Evaluation of the Potential Benefits and Costs of Forming an Economic and Monetary Union, European Economy 44. Brussels: CEC (Commission of the European Communities).

Dullien, S., and Guérot, U. (2012). The Long Shadow of Ordoliberalism: Germany's Approach to the Euro Crisis, Policy Brief. London: European Council on Foreign Relations.

Dyson, K. (2014). *States, Debt, and Power: 'Saints' and 'Sinners' in European History and Integration*. Oxford: Oxford University Press.

Dyson, K. (2013). 'Sworn to Grim Necessity? Imperfections of European Economic Governance, Normative Political Theory and Supreme Emergency', *Journal of European Integration*, 35(3): 207–22.

Eichengreen, B. (2012). 'European Monetary Integration With Benefit of Hindsight', *Journal of Common Market Studies*, 50(S1): 123–36.

Enderlein, H. (2013). 'Das erste Opfer der Krise ist die Demokratie: Wirtschaftspolitik und ihre Legitimation in der Finanzmarktkrise 2008-2013', *Politische Vierteljahresschrift*, 54(4): 714–39.

Enderlein, H., and Fritz-Vannahme, J. (2014). Repair and Prepare: Strengthening Europe's Economies After the Crisis. Gütersloh, Berlin: Bertelsmann Stiftung, Jacques Delors Institut - Berlin.

Enderlein, H., Guttenberg, L., and Spiess, J. (2013). Blueprint for a Cyclical Shock Insurance in the Euro Area, Studies and Reports 100. Paris: Notre Europe - Jacques Delors Institute.

Enderlein, H., Bofinger, P., Boone, L., de Grauwe, P. , Piris, J.-C., Pisani-Ferry, J., Rodrigues, M. J., Sapir, A., and Vitorino, A. (2012). Completing the Euro: A Roadmap Towards Fiscal Union in Europe. Studies and Reports 92. Paris: Notre Europe - Jacques Delors Institute.

Eucken, W. (1990). *Grundsätze der Wirtschaftspolitik*. 6th ed. Tübingen: Mohr Siebeck.

Eucken, W. (1989). 'What Kind of Economic and Social System', in A. T. Peacock, and H. Willgerodt (eds), *Germany's Social Market Economy: Origins and Evolution*. New York: St. Martin's Press, 27–45.

European Commission (2014) [website]. *Annual Macro-Economic Database of the European Commission (AMECO). 1995-2013*. Retrieved from http://ec.europa.eu/economy_finance/ameco/user/serie/SelectSerie.cfm (accessed 12 January 2015).

European Commission (2012). A Blueprint for a Deep and Genuine Economic and Monetary Union. Launching a European Debate. COM(2012) 777 final/2. Brussels: European Commission.

European Commission [website]. *Eurobarometer 1-81.5. 1974-2014*. Retrieved from http://ec.europa.eu/public_opinion/cf/step1.cfm?keyID=62&nationID=11,1,27,28,17,2,16,18,13,32,6,3,4,22,33,7,8,20,21,9,23,31,34,24,12,19,35,29,26,25,5,14,10,30,15,&startdate=1999.04&enddate=2013.05 (accessed 3 Febuary 2015).

European Council (2014). Conclusions - 18 December 2014. EUCO 237/14. Brussels: European Council.

European Parliament (2014). Report on the Enquiry on the Role and Operations of the Troika (ECB, Commission and IMF) With Regard to the Euro Area Programme Countries. A7-0149/2014. Brussels: European Parliament.

Everson, M. (forthcoming). 'Banking on Union: EU Governance Between Risk and Uncertainty', in M. Dawson, H. Enderlein, and C. Joerges (eds), *The Transformation of the European Union: Challenges of Functionality, Design and Democratic Legitimacy*. Oxford: Oxford University Press.

Everson, M. (2013). 'The Fault of (European) Law in (Political and Social) Economic Crisis', *Law and Critique*, 24(2): 107–29.

Everson, M., and Joerges, C. (2013). Who is the Guardian for Constitutionalism in Europe After the Financial Crisis?. 'Europe in Question' Discussion Paper Series 63/2013. London: LSE.

Fabbrini, F. (2014). 'The Euro-Crisis and the Courts: Judicial Review and the Political Process in Comparative Perspective', *Berkeley Journal of International Law*, 32(1): 64–123.

Fabbrini, S. (forthcoming). 'Emerging from the Euro Crisis: The Institutional Dilemma of a Political Union', in M. Dawson, H. Enderlein, and C. Joerges (eds), *The Transformation of the European Union: Challenges of Functionality, Design and Democratic Legitimacy*. Oxford: Oxford University Press.

Fabbrini, S. (2013). 'Intergovernmentalism and Its Limits: Assessing the European Union's Answer to the Euro Crisis', *Comparative Political Studies*, 46(9): 1003–29.

Fasone, C. (2014). 'European Economic Governance and Parliamentary Representation: What Place for the European Parliament?', *European Law Journal*, 20(2): 164–85.

Feld, L. P. (2012). Europa in der Welt von heute: Wilhelm Röpke und die Zukunft der Europäischen Währungsunion. HWWI Policy Paper 70. Hamburg: Hamburgisches WeltWirtschafts Institut.

Feld, L. P. (2011). Ein Scheitern ist nicht eingeplant. Oder: Ordnungspolitische Prinzipien der Europäischen Währungsunion, Impulsreden zur Sozialen Marktwirtschaft. Berlin: Wirtschaftspolitischer Club Deutschland e.V..

Feldstein, M. (2012). 'The Failure of the Euro: The Little Currency that Couldn't', *Foreign Affairs*, 91(1): 105–16.

Feldstein, M. (1997). 'EMU and International Conflict', *Foreign Affairs*, 76(6): 60–76.

Fink-Hooijer, F. (1994). 'The Common Foreign and Security Policy of the European Union', *European Journal of International Law*, 5(1): 173–98.

Fischer-Lescano, A. (2014). 'Competencies of the Troika: Legal Limitations of the Institutions', in N. Bruun, K. Lörcher, and I. Schömann (eds), *The Economic and Financial Crisis and Collective Labour Law in Europe*. Oxford: Hart Publishing, 55–82.

Foucault, M. (2008). *The Birth of Biopolitics: Lectures at the College de France, 1978-1979*. Basingstoke: Palgrave Macmillan.

Frankel, J., and Rose, A. (1998). 'The Endogeneity of the Optimum Currency Area Criteria', *The Economic Journal*, 108(449): 1009–25.

Fratzscher, M. (forthcoming). 'Making the Euro Strive for the Next 100 Years: What is Needed, and What is Missing?', in M. Dawson, H. Enderlein, and C. Joerges (eds), *The Transformation of the European Union: Challenges of Functionality, Design and Democratic Legitimacy*. Oxford: Oxford University Press.

Garton Ash, T. (2012). 'The Crisis of Europe: How the Union Came Together and Why It's Falling Apart', *Foreign Affairs*, 91(5): 2–15.

Garton Ash, T. (1999). 'The Case for Liberal Order', in T. Garton Ash (ed), *History of the Present: Essays, Sketches and Despatches from Europe in the 1990s*. London: Allen Lane.

Genschel, P. and Jachtenfuchs, M. (eds) (2013). *Beyond the Regulatory Polity?: The European Integration of Core State Powers*. Oxford: Oxford University Press.

Gilardi, F. (2014). 'Methods for the Analysis of Policy Independence', in I. Engeli, and C. Rothmayr Allison (eds), *Comparative Policy Studies: Conceptual and Methodological Challenges*. Basingstoke: Palgrave Macmillan, 185–205.

Glasman, M. (1996). *Unnecessary Suffering: Managing Markets Utopia*. London: Verso.

Glossner, C. L. (2010). *The Making of the German Post-War Economy: Political Communication and Public Reception of the Social Market Economy After World War II*. London: Tauris Academic Studies.

Habermas, J. (2014). 'Warum der Ausbau der Europäischen Union zu einer supranationalen Demokratie nötig und wie er möglich ist', *Leviathan*, 42(4): 524–38.

Habermas, J. (2012). 'Die Krise der Europäischen Union im Lichte einer Konstitutionalisierung des Völkerrechts: Ein Essay zur Verfassung Europas', *Zeitschrift für ausländisches und öffentliches Recht und Völkerrecht*, 72(1): 1–44.

Habermas, J. (2011). 'A Pact for or Against Europe?', in U. Guérot, and J. Hénard (eds), *What Does Germany Think About Europe?* London: ECFR, 83–9.

Habermas, J. (2003). 'On Law and Disagreement: Some Comments on "Interpretative Pluralism"', *Ratio Juris*, 16(2): 187–94.

Habermas, J. (2001). 'Constitutional Democracy: A Paradoxical Union of Contradictory Principles?', *Political Theory*, 29(6): 766–81.

Habermas, J. (1996). *Between Facts and Norms: Contributions to a Discourse Theory of Law and Democracy*. Cambridge: MIT Press.

Habermas, J. (1991). *Staatsbürgerschaft und nationale Identität. Überlegungen zur europäischen Zukunft*. St. Gallen: Erker.

Hall, P. A. (2014). 'Varieties of Capitalism and the Euro Crisis', *West European Politics*, 37(6): 1223–43.

Hallstein, W. (1979). *Die Europäische Gemeinschaft*. 5th ed. Düsseldorf: Econ-Verlag.

Hassemer, W. (2012). 'Dalli, dalli, das Haus brennt!', *Frankfurter Allgemeine Zeitung, 28 June 2012*: 35.

Hefftler, C., and Wessels, W. (2013). The Democratic Legitimacy of the EU's Economic Governance and National Parliaments. IAI Working Papers 1313. Rome: Istituto Affari Internazionali.

Heinemann, F. (2013). 'Zwischen "Kernschmelze" und "Fass ohne Boden" - zum Dissens deutscher Ökonomen in der Schuldenkrise', *Zeitschrift für Politik*, 60(2): 201–19.

Hertie School of Governance (ed) (2014). *The Governance Report 2014*. Oxford: Oxford University Press.

Hertie School of Governance (ed) (2013). *The Governance Report 2013*. Oxford: Oxford University Press.

Hinarejos, A. (forthcoming). 'The Role of Courts in the Wake of the Euro Area Crisis', in M. Dawson, H. Enderlein, and C. Joerges (eds), *The Transformation of the European Union: Challenges of Functionality, Design and Democratic Legitimacy*. Oxford: Oxford University Press.

Hinarejos, A. (2013). 'The Court of Justice of the EU and the Legality of the European Stability Mechanism', *Cambridge Law Journal*, 72(2): 237–40.

Höpner, M. (2014). Wie der Europäische Gerichtshof und die Kommission Liberalisierung durchsetzen. Befunde aus der MPIfG-Forschungsgruppe zur Politischen Ökonomie der europäischen Integration. MPIfG Discussion Paper 14/8. Cologne: Max Planck Institute for the Study of Societies.

Innerarity, D. (forthcoming). 'The Inter-Democratic Deficit of the European Union', in M. Dawson, H. Enderlein, and C. Joerges (eds), *The Transformation of the European Union: Challenges of Functionality, Design and Democratic Legitimacy*. Oxford: Oxford University Press.

International Labour Organisation (1956). 'Social Aspect of European Economic Co-operation: Report by a Group of Experts', *International Labour Review*, 74: 99–123.

Iversen, T., and Soskice, D. (2013). A Structural-Institutional Explanation of the Eurozone Crisis. Unpublished Manuscript. Cambridge: Harvard University.

Joerges, C. (2014a). 'Brother, Can You Paradigm?', *International Journal of Constitutional Law*, 12(3): 769–85.

Joerges, C. (2014b). 'Law and Politics in Europe's Crisis: On the History of the Impact of an Unfortunate Configuration', *Constellations*, 21(2): 249–61.

Joerges, C. (2014c). 'Unity in Diversity as Europe's Vocation and Conflicts Law as Europe's Constitutional Form', in R. Nickel, and A. Greppi (eds), *The Changing Role of Law in the Age of Supra- and Transnational Governance*. Baden-Baden: Nomos, 127–76.

Joerges, C. (2013). 'The Timeliness of Direct Democracy in the EU - and the Contest over Atomic Energy in Conflicts-Law Perspective', in K. Lachmayer, J. Busch, J. Kelleher, and G. Turcanu (eds), *International Constitutional Law in Legal Education: Proceedings of the Erasmus Intensive Programme NICLAS 2007-2012*. Baden-Baden: Nomos, 89–100.

Joerges, C. (2009). 'Sozialstaatlichkeit in Europe? A Conflict-of-Laws Approach to the Law of the EU and the Proceduralisation of Constitutionalisation', *German Law Journal*, 10(4): 335–60.

Joerges, C. (2005). 'What is Left of the European Economic Constitution?: A Melancholic Eulogy', *European Law Review*, 30: 461–89.

Joerges, C. (1996). The Market Without a State? States Without Markets? Two Essays on the Law of the European Economy. EUI Working Paper Law 1/96. San Domenico di Fiesole: European University Institute.

Joerges, C. (1994). 'Economic Law, the Nation-State and the Maastricht Treaty', in R. Dehousse (ed), *Europe After Maastricht: An Ever Closer Union?* Munich: Law Books in Europe, 29–62.

Joerges, C., and Rödl, F. (2009). 'Informal Politics, Formalised Law and the "Social Deficit" of European Integration: Reflections After the Judgments of the ECJ in Viking and Laval', *European Law Journal*, 15(1): 1–19.

Joerges, C., and Rödl, F. (2004). '"Social Market Economy" as Europe's Social Model?', in L. Magnusson, and B. Stråth (eds), *A European Social Citizenship?: Preconditions for Future Policies from an Historical Perspective*. Brussels: P. Lang, 125–58.

Joerges, C., and Schmid, C. (2011). 'Towards Proceduralization of Private Law in the European Multi-Level System', in A. Hartkamp, M. Hesselink, E. Hondius, C. Mak, and E. Du Perron (eds), *Towards a European Civil Code*. 4th ed. Nijmegen: Kluwer Law International, 277–310.

Joerges, C., and Weimer, M. (2013). 'A Crisis of Executive Managerialism in the EU: No Alternative?', in G. de Búrca, C. Kilpatrick, and J. Scott (eds), *Critical Legal Perspectives on Global Governance: Liber Amicorum David M Trubek*. Oxford: Hart, 295–322.

Joerges, C., Kjaer, P. F., and Ralli, T. (2011). 'A New Type of Conflicts Law as Constitutional Form in the Postnational Constellation', *Transnational Legal Theory*, 2(2): 153–65.

Judt, T. (2010). *Ill Fares the Land*. New York: Penguin Press.
Kok, W., Bausch, R., FitzGerald, N., Gutiérrez Vegara, A., Hutton, W., Idrac, A.-M., Lundby-Wedin, W., Mirow, T., Moldan, B., Paganetto, L., Rosati, D., Sundbäck, V., and Verzetnitsch, F. (2004). *Facing the Challenge: The Lisbon Strategy for Growth and Employment*. Luxembourg: Office for Official Publications of the European Communities.
Konrad, K. A. (2014). 'Balancing Austerity and Strategies for Growth', *CFA Institute Conference Proceedings Quaterly*, 31(2): 8–15.
Konrad, K. A. (2013). 'Haftungsrisiken und Fehlanreize aus ESM und OMT-Programm', *Wirtschaftsdienst*, 93(7): 431–54.
Krastev, I. (2012). *The Political Logic of Disintegration: Seven Lessons From the Soviet Collapse*. Brussels: Centre for European Policy Studies.
Kundnani, H. (2014). [website] *The Return of the German Question: Why Conflict Between Creditor and Debtor States is Now the Defining Feature of European Politics*. Retrieved from http://blogs.lse.ac.uk/europpblog/2015/01/26/the-return-of-the-german-question-why-conflict-between-creditor-and-debtor-countries-is-now-the-defining-feature-of-european-politics/ (accessed 2 February 2015).
Ladeur, K.-H. (2014). '"Conflicts Law as Europe's Constitutional Form" … and the Conflict of Social Norms as its Infrastructure', in C. Joerges, and C. Glinski (eds), *The European Crisis and the Transformation of Transnational Governance: Authoritarian Managerialism Versus Democratic Governance*. Oxford: Hart Publishing, 383–96.
Lagarde, C. (2011). *An Address to the 2011 International Finance Forum: Beijing, November 9, 2011*. Retrieved from http://www.imf.org/external/np/speeches/2011/110911.htm (accessed 21 January 2015).
Leibfried, S., and Zürn, M. (2005). 'Reconfiguring the National Constellation', in S. Leibfried, and M. Zürn (eds), *Transformations of the State?* Cambridge: Cambridge University Press, 1–36.
Lenoble, J. (1996). 'Law and Undecidability: A New Vision of the Proceduralization of Law', *Cardozo Law Review*, 17(4-5): 935–1004.
MacDougall, D., Biehl, D., Brown, A., Forte, F., Fréville, Y., O'Donoghue, M., and Peeters, T. (1977). Report of the Study Group on the Role of Public Finance in European Integration. Brussels: Commission of the European Communities.
Majone, G. (2014). *Rethinking the Union of Europe Post-Crisis: Has Integration Gone too Far?* Cambridge: Cambridge University Press.
Majone, G. (2012). Rethinking European Integration After the Debt Crisis, Working Paper No. 3/2012. London: UCL European Institute.
Manow, P. (2001a). 'Ordoliberalismus als ökonomische Ordnungstheologie', *Leviathan*, 29(2): 179–98.
Manow, P. (2001b). 'Social Protection, Capitalist Production: The Bismarckian Welfare State and the German Political Economy from the 1880s to the 1990s', Habilitationsschrift. Konstanz: Universität Konstanz.

Marzinotto, B., Wolff, G. B., and Hallerberg, M. (2012). An Assessment of the European Semester. Brussels: Bruegel.

Maurer, A. (2013). From EMU to DEMU: The Democratic Legitimacy of the EU and the European Parliament. IAI Working Papers 13/11. Rome: Istituto Affari Internazionali.

Merkel, A. (2011). *Regierungserklärung von Kanzlerin Merkel zum Europäischen Rat und zum Eurogipfel*. Retrieved from http://www.bundesregierung.de/ContentArchiv/DE/Archiv17/Regierungserklaerung/2011/2011-10-27-merkel-eu-gipfel.html (accessed 30 January 2015).

Mestmäcker, E. J. (2007). *A Legal Theory Without Law*. Tübingen: Mohr Siebeck.

Mestmäcker, E. J. (1973). 'Power, Law and Economic Constitution', *The German Economic Review*, 11(3): 177–92.

Müller-Armack, A. (1966a). 'Die Soziale Marktwirtschaft nach einem Jahrzehnt ihrer Erprobung', in A. Müller-Armack (ed), *Wirtschaftsordnung und Wirtschaftspolitik: Studien und Konzepte zur sozialen Marktwirtschaft und zur Europäischen Integration*. Freiburg: Rombach, 251–65.

Müller-Armack, A. (1966b). 'Die Wirtschaftsordnung sozial gesehen', in A. Müller-Armack (ed), *Wirtschaftsordnung und Wirtschaftspolitik: Studien und Konzepte zur sozialen Marktwirtschaft und zur Europäischen Integration*. Freiburg: Rombach, 171–99.

Müller-Armack, A. (1947). *Wirtschaftslenkung und Marktwirtschaft*. Hamburg: Verlag für Wirtschaft und Sozialpolitik.

Mundell, R. (1961). 'A Theory of Optimum Currency Areas', *American Economic Review*, 51(4): 657–65.

Neumayer, E. (2001). 'Improvement Without Convergence: Pressure on the Environment in European Union Countries', *Journal of Common Market Studies*, 39(5): 927–37.

Neyer, J. (2014). 'Justified Multi-level Parliamentarism: Situating National Parliaments in the European Polity', *The Journal of Legislative Studies*, 20(1): 125–38.

Padoa-Schioppa, T., King, M., Paelinck, J.-H., Papademos, L. D., Pastor, A., and Scharpf, F. W. (1987). *Efficiency, Stability and Equity: A Strategy for the Evolution of the Economic System of the European Community*. Brussels: Commission of the European Communities.

Piedrafita, S., and Blockmans, S. (2014). *Shifting EU Institutional Reform Into High Gear: Report of the CEPS High-Level Group*. Brussels: Centre for European Policy Studies.

Plümper, T., and Schneider, C. J. (2009). 'The Analysis of Policy Convergence, or: How to Chase a Black Cat in a Dark Room', *Journal of European Public Policy*, 16(7): 990–1011.

Polanyi, K. (1937). *Europe To-Day*. London: Worker's Educational Trade Union Committee.

Quaglia, L. (2013). 'Is European Union Governance Ready to Deal With the

Next Crisis?', in H. K. Anheier (ed), *Governance Challenges and Innovations: Financial and Fiscal Governance*. Oxford: Oxford University Press, 63–87.

Rödl, F. (2013). 'Zu Begriff und Perspektiven demokratischer und sozialer Union', in J. Bast, and F. Rödl (eds), *Wohlfahrtsstaatlichkeit und soziale Demokratie in der Europäischen Union: Beiheft zu Europarecht 1/2013*. Baden-Baden: Nomos, 179–204.

Rodrik, D. (2014). *The Future of European Democracy*. Retrieved from https://www.sss.ias.edu/files/pdfs/Rodrik/Commentary/Future-of-Democracy-in-Europe.pdf (accessed 4 February 2015).

Rodrik, D. (2011). *The Globalization Paradox: Democracy and the Future of the World Economy*. London: W. W. Norton.

Ruggie, J. G. (1982). 'International Regimes, Transactions, and Change: Embedded Liberalism in the Postwar Economic Order', *International Organization*, 36(2): 379–415.

Sabel, C. F., and Zeitlin, J. (2012). 'Experimentalism in the EU: Common Ground and Persistent Differences', *Regulation & Governance*, 6(3): 410–26.

Sabel, C. F., and Zeitlin, J. (2008). 'Learning From Difference: The New Architecture of Experimentalist Governance in the EU', *European Law Journal*, 14(3): 271–327.

Scharpf, F. W. (2013). Political Legitimacy in a Non-Optimal Currency Area. MPIfG Discussion Paper 13/15. Cologne: Max Planck Institute for the Study of Societies.

Scharpf, F. W. (2010). 'The Asymmetry of European Integration, or Why the EU Cannot be a "Social Market Economy"', *Socio-Economic Review*, 8(2): 211–50.

Scharpf, F. W. (2003). Problem-Solving Effectiveness and Democratic Accountability in the EU. MPIfG Working Paper 03/1. Cologne: Max Planck Institute for the Study of Societies.

Scharpf, F. W. (2002). 'The European Social Model', *Journal of Common Market Studies*, 40(4): 645–70.

Schelkle, W. (2007). 'EU Fiscal Governance: Hard Law in the Shadow of Soft Law?', *Columbia Journal of European Law*, 13: 705–31.

Scheuerman, W. E. (2000). 'The Economic State of Emergency', *Cardozo Law Review*, 21(5-6): 1869–94.

Schimmelfennig, F., and Winzen, T. (2014). 'Instrumental and Constitutional Differentiation in the European Union', *Journal of Common Market Studies*, 52(2): 354–70.

Streeck, W. (2013). The Politics of Public Debt: Neoliberalism, Capitalist Development, and the Restructuring of the State. MPIfG Discussion Paper 13/7. Cologne: Max Planck Institute for the Study of Societies.

Streeck, W., and Elsässer, L. (2014). Monetary Disunion: The Domestic Politics of Euroland, MPIfG Discussion Paper 14/17. Cologne: Max Planck Institute for the Study of Societies.

Tavlas, G. (1993). 'The "New" Theory of Optimum Currency Areas', *The World Economy*, 16(6): 663–85.

Teubner, G. (2014). 'Transnationale Wirtschaftsverfassung. Franz Böhm und Hugo Sinzheimer jenseits des Nationalstaates', *Zeitschrift für ausländisches öffentliches Recht und Völkerrecht*, 74(4): 733–5.

Tews, K., Busch, P.-O., and Jörgens, H. (2003). 'The Diffusion of New Environmental Policy Instruments', *European Journal of Political Research*, 42(1): 569–600.

The World Bank [website]. *World Development Indicators: Unemployment, Total*. Retrieved from http://data.worldbank.org/indicator/SL.UEM.TOTL.ZS (accessed 3 Feburary 2015).

Tribunal Constitucional Portugal (2013). *Review of the Constitutionality of Norms Contained in the State Budget Law for 2013*, 187/13, Judgment of 5 April 2013.

Trubek, D. M., and Trubek, L. G. (2005). 'Hard and Soft Law in the Construction of Social Europe: The Role of the Open Method of Co-ordination', *European Law Journal*, 11(3): 343–64.

Tuori, K. (2010). 'The Many Constitutions of Europe', in K. Tuori, and S. Sankari (eds), *The Many Constitutions of Europe*. Farnham: Ashgate, 3–30.

Tuori, K., and Tuori, K. (2014). *The Eurozone Crisis: A Constitutional Analysis*. Cambridge: Cambridge University Press.

van Rompuy, H., Barroso, J. M., Juncker, J.-C., and Draghi, M. (2012). Towards a Genuine Economic and Monetary Union: Report by the President of the European Council. Brussels: European Council.

Vanberg, V. (2014). Ordnungspolitik, the Freiburg School and the Reason of Rules. Freiburg Discussion Papers on Constitutional Economics 14/01. Freiburg: Albert-Ludwigs Universität Freiburg im Breisgau.

Viellechner, L. (2012). 'Constitutionalism as a Cipher: On the Convergence of Constitutionalist and Pluralist Approaches to the Globalization of Law', *Goettingen Journal of International Law*, 4(2): 599–623.

von Hayek, F. A. (2002). 'Competition as a Discovery Procedure', *Quarterly Journal of Austrian Economics*, 5(3): 9–23.

von Hayek, F. A. (1989). 'The Pretence of Knowledge', *American Economic Review*, 79(6): 3–7.

Weale, A. (forthcoming). 'Political Legitimacy, Credible Commitment and Euro Governance', in M. Dawson, H. Enderlein, and C. Joerges (eds), *The Transformation of the European Union: Challenges of Functionality, Design and Democratic Legitimacy*. Oxford: Oxford University Press.

Wegmann, M. (2002). *Früher Neoliberalismus und europäische Integration: Interdependenz der nationalen, supranationalen und internationalen Ordnung von Wirtschaft und Gesellschaft (1932-1965)*. Baden-Baden: Nomos.

Weiler, J. H. H. (1994). 'Fin-de-Siècle Europe', in R. Dehousse (ed), *Europe After Maastricht: An Ever Closer Union?* Munich: Law Books in Europe, 203–10.

Wendel, M. (2013). 'Comparative Reasoning and the Making of a Common Constitutional Law: EU-Related Decisions of National Constitutional Courts in a Transnational Perspective', *International Journal of Constitutional Law*, 11(4): 981–1002.

Werner, P., Ansiaux, H., Brouwers, G., Clappier, B., Mosca, U., Schöllhorn, J.-B., and Stammati, G. (1970). Report to the Council and the Commission on the Realisation by Stages of Economic and Monetary Union in the Community: Werner Report. Luxembourg: Council and Commission of the European Communities.

White, J. (2013). 'Emergency Europe', *Political Studies*. Retrieved from http://onlinelibrary.wiley.com/doi/10.1111/1467-9248.12072/abstract (accessed 2 February 2015).

Wigger, A. (2008). *Competition for Competitiveness: The Politics of the Transformation of the EU Competition Regime*. Amsterdam: Vrije Universiteit.

Wilkinson, M. A. (2014). Economic Messianism and Constitutional Power in a 'German Europe': All Courts are Equal, But Some Courts are More Equal than Others. LSE Legal Studies Working Paper 26/2014. London: LSE.

Zeitlin, J. (2005). 'Social Europe and Experimentalist Governance: Towards a New Constitutional Compromise?', in G. de Búrca (ed), *EU Law and the Welfare State: In Search of Solidarity*. Oxford: Oxford University Press, 213–42.

# About the Contributors

**Mark Dawson** (PhD, European University Institute Florence) is Professor of European Law and Governance at the Hertie School of Governance (Berlin, Germany). Before joining the Hertie School, he was from 2009 an Assistant Professor at Maastricht University. He is currently researching on the constitutional implications of EU economic governance and on the enforcement of fundamental rights in the European Union. His book on EU human rights policy, *The Governance of EU Fundamental Rights,* will be published by Cambridge University Press in 2015.

**Henrik Enderlein** (Dr. rer. pol., University of Bremen and Max Planck Institute for the Study of Societies) is Associate Dean and Professor of Political Economy at the Hertie School of Governance (Berlin, Germany). He is also Director of the Jacques Delors Institut - Berlin and has previously worked as an economist at the International and European Relations Directorate of the European Central Bank. His research interests include European integration, international political economy, and economic policy-making.

**Christian Joerges** (Dr. jur., University of Frankfurt) is Professor of Law and Society at the Hertie School of Governance (Berlin, Germany). He is also a Research Professor at the Law Faculty of Bremen University and Co-Director of the Centre of European Law and Politics. Until 2007 he held the chair of European Economic Law at the European University Institute Florence. His research focuses on the Europeanization of economic law, European and transnational regulatory politics, and governance arrangements in constitutional perspectives.

**Liam F. McGrath** (PhD, Essex) is Research Scientist for the Governance Report at the Hertie School of Governance (Berlin, Germany). His research interests are in comparative and international political economy, with particular focus on the causes of and responses to financial crises, as well as political methodology.

The manufacturer's authorised representative in the EU for product safety is
Oxford University Press España S.A. of el Parque Empresarial San Fernando de
Henares, Avenida de Castilla, 2 – 28830 Madrid (www.oup.es/en or product.
safety@oup.com). OUP España S.A. also acts as importer into Spain of products
made by the manufacturer.

www.ingramcontent.com/pod-product-compliance
Ingram Content Group UK Ltd.
Pitfield, Milton Keynes, MK11 3LW, UK
UKHW041259180426
11947UKWH00008B/566